Fitba'

Daft!

An adolescent journey through
the 1972/73 football season

James K. Corstorphine

Published by:

Wast-By Books
Lower Largo
Fife
Scotland

Dedicated to the memory of
East Fife legend

Billy McPhee
1949-2023

Text Copyright © 2024 James K. Corstorphine

All rights reserved

ISBN: 9798332407505

No part of this publication may be reproduced, stored in a retrieval system or transmitted in any form or by any means without the prior permission of the publisher.

By the Same Author

On That Windswept Plain: The First One Hundred Years of East Fife F.C.
(ISBN: 9781976888618)

Black and Gold and Blue:
The East Fife men who pulled on the Scotland jersey
(ISBN: 9798817263855)

Our Boys and the Wise Men: The Origins of Dundee Football Club
(ISBN 9798643521549)

The Earliest Fife Football Clubs
(ISBN: 9781980249580)

East of Thornton Junction: The Story of the FifeCoast Line
(ISBN: 9781976909283)

Wrecked on Fife's Rocky Shores: Dramatic Nineteenth Century Tales of Shipwreck from Around the Coast of Fife
(ISBN:9798759568513)

'Poetry Peter' Smith, the Fisherman Poet of Cellardyke
(ISBN: 9798644727827)

All of the above titles are available in both paperback and Kindle eBook format from Amazon.co.uk

Prologue

During my very early years, it has to be said, I had only a passing interest in football. Having been born and brought up in the East Neuk fishing community of Cellardyke, there were so many other pastimes to while away the hours at weekends and after the school bell had sounded at quarter-to-four. If truth be told, the days weren't really long enough to incorporate a game of football as well. Along with my school chums, endless hours would be spent during the summer months playing with home made boats in rock pools on the local seashore; going swimming both in the sea and at the local open air pool; or fishing for codling and mackerel from my dad's small creel boat.

In fact, some of my happiest childhood memories are of fishing from that boat along with my pals. On many an occasion, when ready to depart from Cellardyke harbour on a fishing trip during those summer evenings, we would hear a shout from the other end of the harbour from one of my friends asking if they could accompany us. My dad never turned anyone away, and I can remember on several occasions there could be as many as ten bairns all seated in that wee creel boat away out to fish for codlings; and not a lifejacket amongst us!

During the dark nights of winter, we would play games under the street lights such as 'Kick the Can'; a pastime not dissimilar to 'Hide and Seek', but one which inevitably brought irate neighbours to their doors after the empty tin can had clattered down the street a few times. It was actually my dad who introduced that particular game to us as it was one he had played with his pals under the gas lamps that lit the Cellardyke streets of the 1930's. In fact, it was not unknown for him to join in with us on the odd occasion!

We rarely kicked a ball back then. We simply had so many other things to occupy our young minds that the need or desire to play football rarely arose.

Another deciding factor regarding football was that we didn't really have anywhere to play the game. All of the open grassland in Cellardyke was of an undulating nature; the nearest proper football pitch being at BankiePark in Anstruther, about a mile away.

My indifferent attitude towards football changed when I took the step up from primary school to the local secondary school, WaidAcademy, in 1970. Suddenly, I had a whole new group of friends, many of whom had a passion for football; and that is when I started to take a keener interest in the game. Of course, one of the first questions that I was asked by my new pals was "what team do you support?"

East Fife, based at BayviewPark in Methil, around sixteen miles to the west of Cellardyke, were the local team; and this was the club that most Cellardyke residents had traditionally followed.

The next closest teams were Dundee and Dundee United, who were based just over twenty miles to the north; and Raith Rovers from Kirkcaldy, around the same distance to the west.

My dad had followed with local tradition and had been a regular at BayviewPark during his younger days until he was 'scunnered' by a poor performance in the late 1950's, after which he never went back. My dad's decision to never set foot in Bayview ever again coincided with the end of East Fife's 'Halcyon Days'; and, just a couple of seasons later, they were languishing in the bottom league.

By the time the question of club loyalty had been thrust upon me, I thought it wise to steer clear of my local side, and decided to pick a team from the upper reaches of the Scottish League. Having decided that 'Old Firm' rivals Rangers and Celtic weren't for me, I looked at the final league table for the previous season, 1969/70, and in my wisdom picked Hibernian, who had finished third, just a point behind Rangers.

It was a decision that I was to regret. The 1970/71 league campaign turned out to be a poor one for the Edinburgh club, who eventually finished in the bottom half of the table.

To be fair, they did reach the third round of the Fairs Cup, where they were knocked out by Liverpool; and they did reach the semi-final of the Scottish Cup; but the 'Hi-bees' also endured some embarrassing defeats to lesser clubs during the course of the season. Being more than a little naïve, and unfamiliar with the rivalry and hatred that existed between certain clubs, I thought that maybe I should switch my allegiance to city rivals Hearts, much to the amusement of my more worldly-wise classmates. However, Hearts weren't faring much better!

Meanwhile, East Fife and Partick Thistle had been battling it out for the Second Division title, and my attentions were inevitably drawn to the fortunes of the team that I should really have been supporting all along. When the dust finally settled at the end of the 1970/71 season, Partick Thistle had emerged victorious in their battle to become Second Division Champions; with East Fife finishing in second place, five points behind the Glasgow side.

These were the days long before promotion play-offs were introduced; and, as the teams who finished in the top two places in the Second Division table were both automatically promoted, this meant that top league football would be returning to Methil for the first time in well over a decade.

It was during the following season, 1971/72, that I developed a real craving for all things related to East Fife and to football in general. In other words, I became a football fanatic.

Every Saturday evening during the football season I would make the long trek from Cellardyke to Brattesani's shop in Anstruther to buy my Sporting Post, which was a weekly sports paper printed in Dundee and brought to Anstruther by way of the No. 355 passenger 'bus service that slowly wended its way across the TayBridge and around the coast, dropping off copies of the much revered newspaper along the way.

I would sit late into the evening studying the latest results and league standings from both the Scottish and English leagues before perusing the following week's fixtures.

My dad, naturally, tried to dissuade me from such a pastime, insisting that I was just filling my head full of useless information that would be of no use to anyone. He obviously thought that my spare time would be much better spent doing school homework and other 'more meaningful' pursuits.

When he spied me with my head buried in the Sporting Post, he would sing that traditional song:

> *"Oh, for he's fitba' crazy,*
> *He's fitba' daft;*
> *Oh, the fitba' it has robbed him o'*
> *The wee bit sense he had!"*

This only served to make me even more determined to indulge in my hobby, however, and throughout the 1971/72 season I followed East Fife's progress intensely as they battled to maintain their First Division status. Fortunately, East Fife survived that first season back in the big time, but only just, as they avoided relegation by the skin of their teeth.

And that is how I became a 'dyed in the wool' East Fife supporter. I even kept a scrapbook full of match reports accompanied by the occasional photograph snipped from the Sporting Post, the Dundee Courier or the East Fife Mail, as well as from various other newspapers.

However, for some considerable time after pledging my allegiance to the 'Black and Gold', I was forced to remain an 'armchair fan' due to certain circumstances which will be fully explained within the pages of this book!

1

I just couldn't wait for the 1972/73 football season to begin. This was to be East Fife's second season back in the top flight of Scottish Football; and, as it eventually turned out, this was the season destined to become forever etched on my memory.

It was to be special in so many ways; through memorable performances at BayviewPark against some of the biggest clubs in Scotland; and through the great atmosphere that existed at East Fife's home matches as they strived to bring back the glory days that the club had enjoyed during the decade that followed the Second World War. For a football daft laddie only just into his early teens, these were great times!

It could have been so different, however, had matters not gone East Fife's way as the previous campaign reached its conclusion. When Celtic clinched their seventh consecutive First Division title at Bayview on 15th April 1972 with a three-nil victory, a good number of the East Fife faithful reluctantly resigned themselves to the probability that their favourites' return to the top flight was to last just one season.

That evening, as usual, I studied the following week's fixtures, and worked out what the chances were that my favourite club could avoid relegation to the Second Division. This, of course, involved a lot of arithmetical calculations as well as assessing probability based on certain data that had been gathered throughout the course of the season. In other words, I was spending my Saturday night practising my mathematical skills.

According to dad, of course, I was just wasting my time filling my mind with useless information that would be of no use to anyone.

But what I was doing, on a Saturday night no less, was exactly the same as school homework, so surely he should be encouraging me and not criticising. Just what, exactly, was his problem?

The gist of what I worked out that evening was this. With only two games remaining, both away from home against Motherwell and St. Johnstone, both of whom were sitting in the top half of the league table, escaping the drop looked like a very tall order indeed!

At that stage, the men in black and gold were sitting third bottom of the league with the same points total and games played as second bottom Clyde, and four ahead of bottom team Dunfermline Athletic, who had played two games less.

Of their four remaining fixtures, Dunfermline had three 'winnable' home fixtures left; against Morton, Clyde and Dundee United, but had a tricky away meeting with Rangers to negotiate. All things considered, it certainly looked like East Fife had the toughest run-in to the end of the season!

Matters went from bad to worse during the following midweek when Dunfermline beat Morton to close the gap on East Fife to just two points. However, on Saturday 22nd April, against all the odds, East Fife pulled off a surprise single goal victory over St. Johnstone in Perth thanks to a cracking 25-yard rocket from the legendary Billy McPhee. With Dunfermline and Clyde sharing the spoils at East EndPark on the same afternoon, the league table in that Saturday evening's Sporting Post made for much happier reading. Suddenly there was a glimmer of light at the end of the tunnel.

With just one game to play, East Fife were a point ahead of Clyde and three ahead of Dunfermline, who still had one game 'in hand'. However, with Dunfermline having to face Rangers at Ibrox during the following midweek, surely their game 'in hand' would be nullified?

At least that's what I thought.

To everyone's surprise, the 'Pars' pulled off a shock 4-3 victory against the team sitting third in the league table; which meant that, going into the final round of matches, East Fife had just a single point advantage over the two teams beneath them.

On the final Saturday, if either Dunfermline or Clyde picked up full points at home, then East Fife would have to gain at least a point against Motherwell at FirPark in order to save their First Division status.

In the event, the men in black and gold secured a 1-1 draw at Motherwell thanks to a Joe Hughes equaliser on the half-hour mark after the home side had taken an early lead, and East Fife escaped the drop. Those supporters who had just two weeks earlier been resigned to relegation could now look forward to the following season with renewed enthusiasm!

It was with a spring in my step that I made the two-mile round trip from Cellardyke to Brattesani's in Anstruther that Saturday night for my Sporting Post.

Brattesani's was a traditional tobacconist, sweet shop and ice cream parlour situated in the town's Shore Street, looking out on to the harbour, and was a popular place on a Saturday evening.

On entering the shop, one couldn't help but notice the sweet aroma of the ice cream that was made on the premises. On the left hand side was a huge wall-mounted mirror emblazoned with 'Anstruther Aerated Water Company' in fancy lettering, in front of which sat a table where locals passed the time playing cards whilst enjoying a smoke. I was once told that an American tourist had offered proprietor Jimmy Brattesani an eye-watering amount of money for the mirror, but the offer was turned down as the mirror had been there for as long as anyone could remember and the shop just wouldn't look the same without it.

The wall on the opposite side was completely covered with a glass case, inside of which was displayed an array of every type of smoker's pipe you could imagine. In front of this case there was another table, around which another 'card school' would generally be assembled.

I should point out, however, that no money exchanged hands during these card games as they were played purely for fun. At least that's what I was told!

It was said that 'Jimmy' Brattesani (real name Manigeldo Dominico Brattesani) made the best ice cream for miles around, and few who tasted this delicacy would dispute that claim. Throughout my childhood my dad would regularly treat the family to an ice cream cone on a sunny Sunday afternoon, which we ate whilst having a walk down the pier to look at the fishing boats in Anstruther harbour. Rather than have a cone, dad would always enjoy a 'Chocolate Slider', which was a considerably more expensive treat consisting of an ice cream wafer containing chocolate and nougat.

On a Saturday evening, there was always a queue in the shop after the Sporting Post had been delivered; and, on some occasions, if you weren't quick enough, they could be sold out before you reached the counter. I was always there in plenty of time, though, and on the final Saturday of the 1971/72 season I managed to procure my copy as usual.

Sure enough, there it was on the front page, the final First Division league table, which confirmed that the men in black and gold had escaped relegation. They had attained a final position of third from bottom; a point ahead of Clyde, who could only draw with Airdrieonians; and two ahead of Dunfermline Athletic, who had lost at home to Dundee United.

At school on the Monday morning, there was a buzz in the air. East Fife's top league survival was the main topic of discussion amongst my class mates; and even those who normally followed the fortunes of Celtic and Rangers enthused about the fact that their favourites would be visiting Methil once again during the 1972/73 season.

The only voices of negativity came from a couple of Raith Rovers supporters who were totally envious of East Fife's top flight status; their side having failed yet again to make a return to the First Division.

During the summer of 1972, like any other summer, I spent most of the school holidays either swimming or fishing during the day; then hanging out with my pals in the evenings along at Anstruther harbour, where we played the 'one-armed-bandits' or rode the 'Waltzer' at the side shows which traditionally occupied the middle pier during the summer months.

As the weeks wore on, however, I started to get a bit fed up with that routine, and decided to explore a bit further afield on my bike. It was on one of these cycle runs that I found myself in the nearby village of St. Monans, where I decided to call on one of my school chums, fellow East Fife fan Donald, who lived down near the Old Kirk at the western end of the village.

Donald was more than pleased to see me; not only because he was at a bit of a loose end, like myself, but because he had something to show me. His dad, like my dad, had a dislike for football; and, because of this, neither of us had ever woken up on Christmas morning to the joy of discovering that Santa had honoured our lettered request for a Subbuteo table football set.

Donald had managed to overcome this mutual deprivation, however, by making his own table football game. To make the players, he had raided his mum's sewing box for old buttons, to which he attached pieces of card that had been fashioned to the shape of football players, which he had cut from an old shoe box.

He had then drawn out a football pitch on a large sheet of paper, on to which were attached goals that had also been made from card cut from the shoe box. A small button was used for the ball, and the game was played in a fashion not dissimilar to the game of 'tiddley-winks'.

Unlike Subbuteo, Donald's version had the distinct advantage that, by using coloured felt pens, the players could not only be made to wear up-to-date East Fife jerseys, but each individual player could be given their appropriate hair style. Here, in front of me, were miniature versions of the East Fife team from the 1971/72 season, including the likes of Billy McPhee, Peter McQuade and Graham Honeyman. It was pure genius!

Obviously, East Fife needed opponents, so Donald had also made two other teams; the Scotland international team, which included the likes of Denis Law, Billy Bremner and Peter Lorimer; and local amateurs St. Monans Swallows!

We played table football for a couple of hours, before our fun was brought to an end when Donald's mum shouted up the stairs to say that it was now late afternoon and about time I was heading for home.

I pedaled furiously in order to get back to Cellardyke in time for tea; and, all the way home, all I could think about was how I was going to make my own version of Donald's table football game.

That evening, I managed to procure the necessary materials, and set about the task of cutting out two teams of eleven football players from an old shoe box.

However, this task turned out to be harder than I had anticipated; and, by the time I had made ten players, my fingers were starting to hurt due to the pressure of having to squeeze hard on the scissor handles to cut the cardboard.

In order to get the first game under way I was going to have to cut out a further twelve players, then all twenty-two were going to have to be coloured in; have their hair styled; then be attached to the buttons. And it looked like I might be running out of buttons.

It was at this point that I decided to cut corners and make my table football game a five-a-side version!

2

I was brought up to appreciate that money doesn't grow on trees; and that, if I wanted the little luxuries in life, then I was going to have to earn money to buy them. My parents weren't poor by any means; in fact they both had good jobs; but it was drilled into me from an early age that I couldn't expect to ask for and be given anything that my little heart desired. In hindsight, this was no bad thing, and instilled an appreciation of the value of money into me which has served me well throughout my life.

And so, as soon as I was old enough, I went looking for a job, and ended up working as a paper boy for a newsagent who had a shop in Anstruther's Shore Street. The job didn't exactly pay well, but it had a great perk in that I could read comics and magazines for free as I walked the streets, before posting the half-read publications through the appropriate letter boxes.

The football magazines that I delivered were the 'Shoot' and the 'Goal', both of which mainly featured English football, but were still a great read for a young fitba' daft teenager. They did have some articles of Scottish interest, though, and occasionally the team photo in the centrefold would be of a Scottish side. These magazines were usually well thumbed before their intended recipients had a chance to read them!

My other love was music, and at that time there were three tabloid-sized weekly music newspapers which were delivered on Friday mornings. They were the New Musical Express; Sounds; and Melody Maker. I was fortunate in that I had to deliver all three on my round; and, through the pages of these publications, I was able to keep up to date with all the latest happenings in the music world as well as study the latest single and album chart positions.

The New Musical Express occasionally gave away free seven-inch floppy singles, which were stuck to the front page. However, these could easily become detached, and sometimes went missing from the copies that I had to deliver. I believe I still have a couple of these records, one by Alice Cooper and one by the Faces, somewhere in the attic!

Although I wouldn't have admitted it to my friends at the time, the Jackie magazine, which was aimed primarily at young teenage girls, was also a good read, especially the problem page. I remember being so engrossed in this particular column one morning just before posting the magazine through a letter box that I didn't notice the door opening and a young girl, who I knew from school, staring at me from the doorway with a look that could kill. Without saying a word, she snatched the magazine from my grasp and slammed the door in my face. Was she the anonymous writer to the Cathy and Claire problem page impatiently awaiting her reply? Unfortunately I will never know.

The eagerly awaited new football season finally arrived on 29th July 1972, when East Fife kicked off their preparation for the forthcoming campaign with a friendly against Sheffield Wednesday at Bayview, where a crowd of 4,564 turned out to see the visitors emerge victors by three-goals-to-one.

Just days after the Sheffield game, the Methil men embarked on a two-match tour of the Netherlands, where Dordrecht were beaten 2-0 on 2nd August; before FC Haarlem, who had only just been promoted to Netherlands' top flight, the Eredivisie, were defeated by three goals to two four days later.

Back in Methil, East Fife completed their programme of pre-season friendlies with a no-scoring draw against another top Dutch side, ADO Den Haag, who had finished the previous season in the Eredivisie just five places behind Dutch League Champions and reigning European Cup holders Ajax. Having given a good account of themselves against some of the top teams in the Netherlands, things were certainly looking promising for the football season that lay ahead!

The Bayview

Printed and Published by ARTIGRAF OF BUCKHAVEN.   Price 5p.

Souvenir Programme

EAST FIFE
VERSUS
SHEFFIELD WEDNESDAY

PRE-SEASON FRIENDLY

SATURDAY 29th. JULY 1972

AT 3p.m.

BAYVIEW PARK, METHIL.

EAST FIFE FOOTBALL CLUB OFFICIAL PROGRAMME

Competitively, the 1972/73 season started with the League Cup sectional fixtures, where the Scottish League sides were drawn into groups of four or five to compete for a place in the knock-out stages. This had been the accepted format of the competition ever since it had been introduced shortly after the Second World War; and, almost every year since then, the League Cup sectional fixtures had taken up the first six competitive matches of the season. East Fife had, at that time, won the League Cup no fewer than three times during the twenty-seven years that the competition had been in existence; a record bettered only by both halves of the 'Old Firm' and Hearts.

The first League Cup sectional fixture of the season was against newly-promoted Arbroath at Bayview on Saturday 12th August 1972, where a crowd of just under four thousand looked on as Billy McPhee and Mike Green, a recent signing from Blackpool, found the net in a 2-1 victory.

That evening, I made my usual long trek to Anstruther to buy the Sporting Post, which was now going to be an infinitely more interesting read than it had been during the long hot summer, when the news reports were all about cricket, golf, and other such boring pastimes.

As usual, the No.355 from Dundee drew up at the 'bus stop opposite the Murray Library at precisely seven o'clock, where the eagerly awaited bundle of newspapers was handed to a willing volunteer, who proceeded briskly along Shore Street to Brattesani's. Once placed on the counter inside the shop, the string holding the roll of papers was cut as an impatient and excited gathering looked on, all desperate to see the afternoon's results and read the match reports.

We didn't have the luxury of mobile 'phones and the internet in those days to keep us up to date with developments in the world of football throughout Saturday afternoon; and those individuals who had missed the tea time results service on television or radio would have no idea how that day's football matches had finished until they picked up their copy of the Sporting Post.

The Bayview

Printed & Published by Artigraf Printing Company, Buckhaven. Price 5p.

George Young, the Albion 'keeper hardly gets a look at the ball as it sizzles by the post.

WEDNESDAY, AUGUST 23rd, 1972.

BAYVIEW PARK, METHIL.

EAST FIFE
VERSUS
CELTIC

EAST FIFE FOOTBALL CLUB OFFICIAL PROGRAMME

For me, Saturdays had a purpose once again, and I spent that evening engrossed in my much loved pursuit of studying football results, match reports, and forthcoming fixtures.

Four days after the Arbroath game, on the evening of Wednesday 16th August, the Fife travelled through to Glasgow to face Celtic in the second of their six sectional League Cup fixtures. It all looked very promising for the Methil men during the first half, when Kevin Hegarty netted the opening goal after half-an-hour's play following good work from Mike Green. During the second half, Celtic stepped up a gear, and eventually managed to equalise through promising youngster Kenny Dalglish with nineteen minutes to go. The home side then pressed for the winner as darkness fell (the Celtic Park floodlights were being upgraded and were temporarily out of action), but the East Fife defence held firm and the game ended all-square at a goal apiece.

On the following Saturday, Division Two side Stirling Albion were the visitors to Bayview, where a crowd of well over four thousand turned up fully expecting a comfortable win for the home side following their promising start to the season. This game, however, turned out to be something of a damp squib, with neither side managing to find the net.

The series of League Cup sectional fixtures was now at the half-way stage, and East Fife were sitting second in their four-team section on four points; a point behind leaders Celtic; a point ahead of Stirling Albion; and three points clear of bottom club Arbroath.

On Wednesday 23rd August, Celtic were the visitors to Bayview for a match that was, in all probability, going to decide the eventual winners of the League Cup section. With a crowd of almost 10,000 looking on, the visitors took the lead through Bobby Lennox just before half-time, before a brace from Kenny Dalglish gave the visitors a three-goal advantage with fifteen minutes remaining. East Fife just refused to give up, however, and with little over ten minutes left on the clock Kevin Hegarty latched on to a pass from Billy McPhee before coolly slotting the ball home.

Then, four minutes from the end, it was that man Hegarty who found the net again, following a bad clearance from Danny McGrain, to set up a grandstand finish. But it was not to be, and Celtic held out to win by three goals to two.

The disappointment of that first competitive defeat of the season was then exacerbated three days later with a three-goal defeat to Arbroath (who had so far failed to take a single point from any of their fixtures) at Gayfield, thanks to a Kenny Payne brace either side of a Billy Pirie penalty. The fact that the 'Red Lichties' had scored just one goal and conceded seven in their previous two home matches made this result even harder to take.

How could it be possible for my favourite team be jostling for pole position with Celtic in midweek, then just three days later be beaten by the worst team in the group? It was with an air of despondency that I scanned the final round of League Cup fixtures in that Saturday evening's paper. East Fife faced a trip to Annfield to face Stirling Albion on Wednesday evening for their final League Cup sectional fixture; whilst Celtic, now confirmed as group winners, had a home game against Arbroath.

With two teams qualifying from each section, victory at Stirling would still see the Fife through to the second round. But it was going to be a tall order, as the home side also had a chance to progress in the competition and would be equally determined to secure victory. In the event, the Methil men came out with all guns blazing at Annfield; and, after only eight minutes play, a speculative shot from Billy McPhee crept just inside the post to open the scoring. Try as they might, the home side just couldn't break down a stubborn East Fife defence, and when Doug Dailey doubled the advantage just minutes into the second half the game was as good as won.

Having now qualified from their section along with Celtic for the knock-out stages of the tournament, there was a belief amongst some supporters, especially the eternally optimistic youngsters of my age, that the Methil men could be on the road to a Hampden final once again!

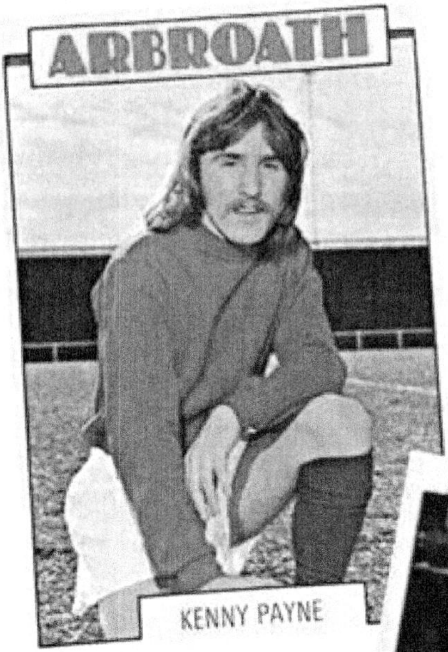
ARBROATH
KENNY PAYNE

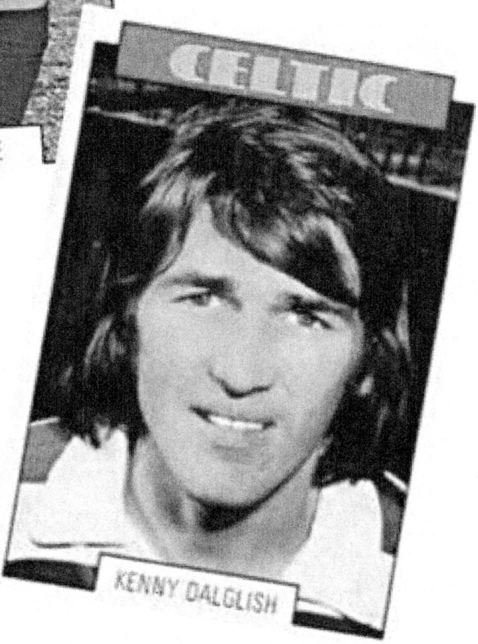
CELTIC
KENNY DALGLISH

The Fife were rewarded for their efforts with a two-legged second round tie against Partick Thistle, the League Cup holders, who had famously thumped Celtic by four-goals-to-one in the previous season's final. However, the first leg of that clash wasn't due for another three weeks, and my focus was now on the long-awaited start of the league campaign which was due to get under way in just three days time on Saturday 2nd September.

I just couldn't wait!

EAST FIFE

BILLY McPHEE

EAST FIFE

KEVIN HEGARTY

3

As I previously mentioned, to the great frustration of my parents, my young teenage mind was occupied almost constantly with anything and everything related to the game of football, much to the detriment of my school studies. If my exams had been on the subject of East Fife Football Club; or, indeed, anything to do with Scottish Football at that time, then I would surely have passed with flying colours and been sent to the top of the class. My mind was rarely on other things.

Even during the school dinner break, I would race with my pals from the WaidAcademy down Anstruther's Rodger Street to Lindsay Berwick's sweetie shop, where my dinner money would either be blown on a football magazine; or, more often than not, spent on a small package containing four football picture cards and a small strip of pink bubble gum.

These picture cards, which were a bit like the 'Panini' stickers of today, were of players who played for Scottish First Division clubs, as well as a few Scotland internationalists who were at the time plying their trade south of the border, including the likes of Leeds United's Peter Lorimer, Manchester United's Willie Morgan, or Chelsea's St Monans-born winger Charlie Cooke.

The hobby of collecting these cards in order to obtain a full set was extremely popular amongst my classmates; and, after comparing the four cards with those I already had in my pocket, the bubble gum would be chewed and popped as I traded 'doublers' with my pals outside the shop.

A picture card of almost every East Fife player was available to collect, and I can vividly remember those of Billy McPhee, Peter McQuade, Walter Borthwick, Bobby Duncan and Davie Clarke to name but a few.

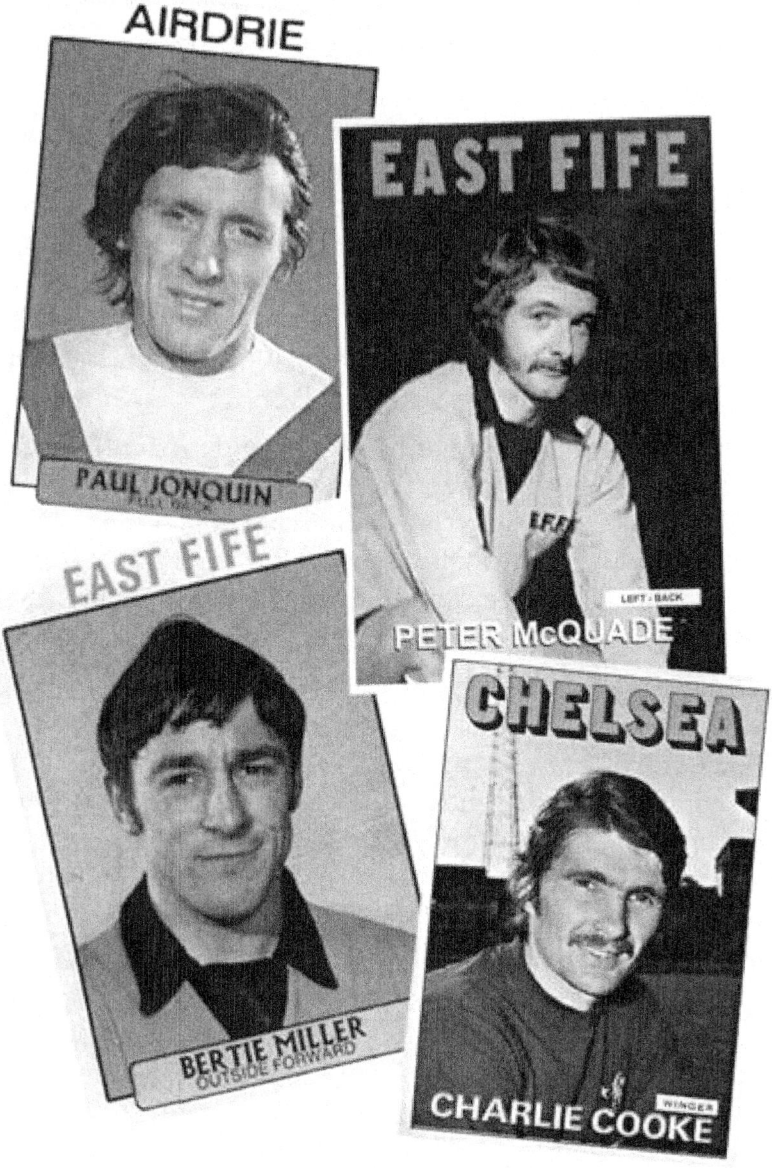
AIRDRIE
PAUL JONQUIN
EAST FIFE
LEFT-BACK
PETER McQUADE
EAST FIFE
BERTIE MILLER
OUTSIDE FORWARD
CHELSEA
WINGER
CHARLIE COOKE

Many years later, Peter McQuade told me that they were all paid the princely sum of one pound each if they agreed to stay behind after training to have their picture taken when the photographer called!

For some reason, there seemed to be an abundance of certain cards, and I remember Airdrie's Paul Jonquin being so commonplace (sometimes two in the same packet) that he was impossible to get rid of. Other cards, including that of East Fife's Bertie Miller, who had departed for Aberdeen at the start of the 1971/72 season, were harder to find. I suppose searching for such rarities are what made the hobby so exciting.

The start of the league campaign was what I looked forward to most of all, however, and on Saturday 2nd September that day finally arrived with the visit of Morton to Bayview. With the Greenock side having ended the previous season just two points ahead of East Fife, a closely fought battle was anticipated, and the crowd of 3,680 who lined the Bayview terraces were not to be disappointed. The Fife raced to a 3-1 half time lead, but they had Morton full-backs Tony Shevlane and Archie Hayes to thank for two of the counters; both of the defenders having put the ball into their own net. East Fife's third was a penalty scored by Billy McPhee.

Morton, who had netted seven goals against Cowdenbeath in their previous outing, came out for the second half determined to make amends for their first-half errors; but despite giving it their best shot and finding the net twice, they couldn't turn the match around; and the men in black and gold eventually ran out victors by four goals to three to take full points; the all-important fourth goal having been scored by Walter Borthwick.

It was a winning start to the league campaign, and that Saturday evening's paper made for interesting reading. Yes, perhaps only one game had been played, but in the mind of a young football fan like myself East Fife were deservedly sitting in the top half of the league table; several places in front of Rangers, who had surprisingly lost their opening day fixture to Ayr United at SomersetPark.

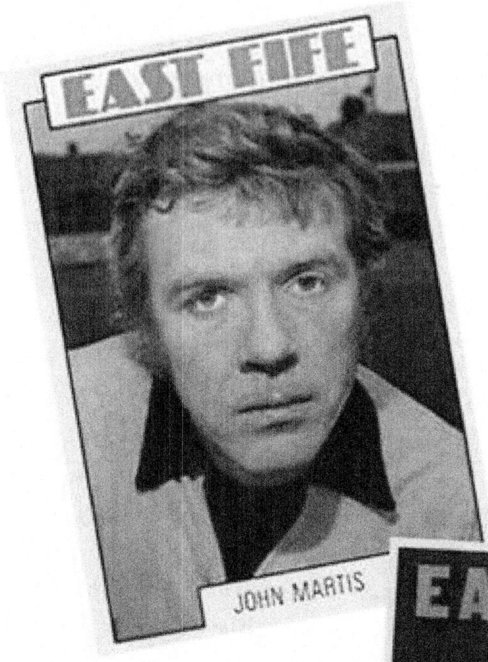
EAST FIFE
JOHN MARTIS

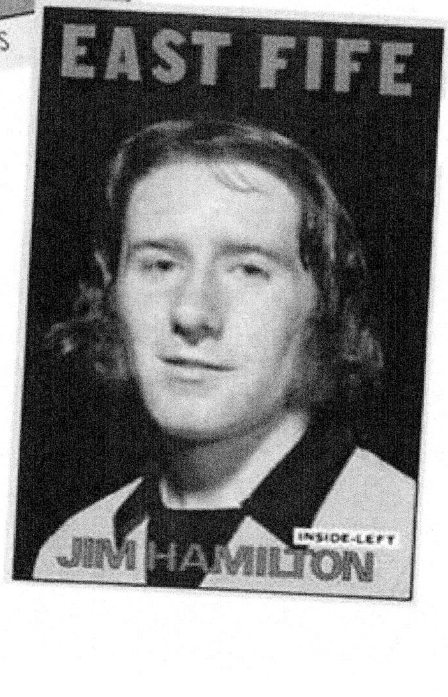
EAST FIFE
INSIDE-LEFT
JIM HAMILTON

If a team like Ayr (who had fought out the previous league season almost on a par with East Fife) could beat Rangers, then surely similar results awaited the Methil men?

A perusal of 'Next Week's Fixture Card' revealed that East Fife's next league match was away to Arbroath on the following Saturday. Surely full points would be taken from these 'minnows' who had only just been promoted from the Second Division, and had lost their opening day league fixture to Falkirk? The fact that East Fife had lost by three goals without reply to these so-called 'minnows' just four weeks earlier seemed to have completely eluded my muddled young mind!

My concentration whilst studying the results, league tables and fixtures was rudely interrupted at this point by my dad, who had spent the early part of the evening watching television highlights from the 1972 Olympic Games in Munich.

"I think its aboot time you spent fewer hours on useless pastimes like studyin' fitba' results and spent mair time concentratin' on getting' yer physical condition intae shape", he advised me. *"Maybe then you would be able tae compete in athletics events at school instead o' jist bein' a stiffie".*

He touched a nerve with that one, but I decided not to rise to the bait. The fact that I was actually quite a good swimmer and had competed at inter-school level in swimming competitions seemed to have eluded him. He also seemed to have forgotten that I played for the school rugby team.

"I've just been watchin' real athletes competin' in the track and field events", he continued. *"Real sportsmen, no' like these fitba' players that ye seem tae hold in such high esteem. A real sportsman is something that you'll never be if ye always hae yer heid buried in the Sportin' Post".*

That was the final straw. I could hold back no longer.

"I could beat you at runnin' any day!" I retorted.

I should perhaps mention at this point that dad had actually fancied himself as a bit of a runner in his younger days. Whilst doing his National Service back in the early 1950's, he had apparently competed in an army athletics event held at Charlton Athletic's football ground, The Valley, when he was stationed at barracks somewhere in London. Or so he claimed.

"Let's see ye prove it then", he gleefully replied.

And so, on the following evening, we agreed on a route of around half a mile through the local streets, starting and finishing at the front door of our house. My mum, who seemed to find the whole thing rather amusing, signalled the start of the race, and immediately my dad shot away at breakneck speed.

I have to admit that I was surprised at how fast he was for someone in his early forties, but I managed to keep pace with him all the way around the agreed course. Then, when we entered the home straight, I sprinted away and won the race by quite a considerable distance.

As I tried to catch my breath, I turned around to see where dad was, and was surprised to see that he was still quite a way back and was walking slowly up the street.

When he eventually arrived back at the front door of the house, he looked me up and down, grimaced, and lamented: *"of a' the times fur ma auld hamstring injury tae play up!"*

4

A week after their opening day league victory over Greenock Morton, East Fife made the short journey north for their second league fixture of the season against newly-promoted Arbroath at GayfieldPark. Despite the fact that the Methil men had been humbled by the 'Red Lichties' in a League Cup fixture at the same venue during the previous month, confidence was high that their winning start to the league campaign would be maintained.

The day of the match against Arbroath dawned bright but unseasonably chilly; and, although it was still officially summertime, the overnight temperature had dipped to an incredible minus seven degrees in Aviemore, and snow was reported to have been falling heavily on the Scottish mountains.

Now, anyone who has ever visited GayfieldPark will testify to it being an extremely cold place to watch a game of football at the best of times, being as it is within a stone's throw of the North Sea. Well, I can't say for certain if the unseasonable conditions had anything to with East Fife's performance, but the fact of the matter is that, following a dour first half during which neither side created many chances, the home side eventually emerged victors by a single goal.

The disappointment of that unexpected defeat (in the eyes of the ever-optimistic young football fan) was soon forgotten, however, as the following week's league fixture, against Hibernian at Bayview, was looked forward to with renewed enthusiasm.

Just over eight months earlier, on 3rd January 1972, the 'Hibees' had been put to the sword at Bayview in what had been East Fife's first home league victory over the Edinburgh side since 1952. Surely they could do it again?

There's something I should now confess. Although I had, for a couple of seasons now, considered myself to be a 'dyed in the wool' East Fife fan, I hadn't actually been to an East Fife match. In fact, I had never been to a senior football match of any description!

There were two reasons for this. The first was that my dad wouldn't take me because he had given up on East Fife some twenty years earlier, and I had no uncles or other older family members living locally that I could go with.

The second reason was my father's belief that all football grounds had become dens of violence since he had last attended a football match all these years ago, and he didn't want me to get caught up in a terracing brawl.

Considering the violence that did occasionally erupt between rival sets of football fans during the early 1970's, there was perhaps some justification in his view on the matter. However, when I consider the fact that he didn't seem to have any problem with some of the other antics that I got up to with my school chums at that time, like abseiling down the pier wall at Cellardyke harbour on the end of an old piece of rope, with the tide out and only jagged rocks to break my fall, it seems rather absurd that he thought attending a football match in Methil was a more dangerous pastime.

Another rather dangerous activity that we Cellardyke youngsters engaged in back then was the construction of wooden rafts made from old fish boxes. The boxes were turned upside down and nailed together before empty one-gallon oil cans were inserted underneath as buoyancy to keep the raft afloat. During the school summer holidays, if the sea was calm enough, it was not unknown for me to paddle right out of Cellardyke harbour to go fishing for flounders over the sandbank which was located about twenty or so yards beyond the harbour mouth. With no lifejacket, I shudder to think what might have happened if the weather had turned!

The hobby of raft building became so popular locally that raft races were held in Anstruther harbour as part of the 'Sea Food

Festival' during the early 1970's, and I can proudly say that I finished runner-up on two occasions. I hadn't even entered my teenage years at the time I indulged in my raft building and sailing activities, but my dad seemed to have no objections to this dangerous leisure activity, despite my age, and had even stood on the East Pier at Anstruther to cheer me on when I competed in the races.

Surely, then, as I was now a teenager (if only for a matter of months), he wouldn't have a problem with me boarding the No. 355 'bus service to Leven on my own on a Saturday afternoon, from where I could make the short walk up to BayviewPark?

I was even in a position to fund the whole venture myself, having risen regularly at six-thirty every morning for the past year or so to carry out my paper round, for which I was paid the princely sum of eighty pence per week. However, my timid request for permission to attend the forthcoming home game against Hibs was refused.

"Ye're no' goin', and there's an end tae it!" he told me firmly, before adding: *"Ye'll end up getting' hit on the heid wi' a bottle. Fitba' grunds are dangerous places nooadays. No' like when I used tae go".*

And so, that was that. I was just going to have to spend another Saturday afternoon watching our local amateur side, Anster United, at BankiePark, where even a keenly fought local derby against Pittenweem Rovers didn't spark off any unsavoury incidents amongst the rival factions of supporters apart from the odd difference of opinion and heated exchange of words!

As the amateur matches traditionally kicked off earlier than the senior games, normally at two o'clock, there was usually time to run home after the game to catch the half-time scores on the radio; and so, on the afternoon of the East Fife v Hibs match, I rushed home from Bankie Park to learn that there had been no scoring at Bayview.

So far, so good. There was still a possibility that full points could be won; and, with both sides currently having one victory and two league points under their belts, victory would see East Fife leapfrog the 'Hibees' and reclaim a place in the upper reaches of the league table. Sadly, it was not to be.

To my immense disappointment, it was the Edinburgh side who took full points thanks to a late second-half strike from Alan Gordon, and that Saturday night's league table showed that East Fife had slipped a little further down the table to eleventh place with three games played.

I was still 'in the huff' with my dad as I studied the pages of my Sporting Post that evening, and found it extremely irritating when he interrupted my perusal of the match reports by announcing, with an 'I told you so' look on his face, that there had been a serious outbreak of fighting that afternoon at the Derby County v Birmingham City match, where hundreds of Birmingham supporters had invaded the pitch and charged towards the Derby supporters at the other end of the ground.

Several arrests had been made; a scenario which, in his opinion, could so easily have occurred at the East Fife v Hibs game. It looked like my first visit to Bayview would not be happening for some considerable time!

5

We were now several weeks into the 1972/73 football season, and it was an incredibly exciting time for me and for and my school chums. Every Friday, when school finished, we would walk home comparing and swapping football cards whilst enthusiastically chatting about that weekend's forthcoming matches. Similarly, on our way back to school on the Monday morning, the topic of conversation was always about Saturday's football results and the games that we had watched on the television highlight programmes.

Of course, live football matches on television were few and far between in those days, and we had to make do with two highlights programmes, which were BBC's Sportsreel on a Saturday night followed by STV's Scotsport on the Sunday afternoon, presented by the legendary Arthur Montford.

Highlights from only one game were shown on each programme; and, even then, there was the odd occasion when the only camera in use had failed half way through the match, which meant that some of the goals had been missed. In addition to this, if during the winter months Scotsport started with Arthur Montford seated inside an ice rink, you could rest assured that the game STV had intended covering had been cancelled and we were going to have to suffer an hour of curling instead!

One regular feature that I always looked forward to on Scotsport was a ten minute slot allocated to the legendary Bob Crampsey, who was widely acknowledged at the time as 'the nation's foremost football historian'. I would sit enthralled as Bob recounted Scottish football tales from the halcyon days of the 1950s or earlier in a knowledgeable and often humorous way.

I had the great pleasure of meeting Bob Crampsey at a function many years later, when he asked me what team I followed.

When I told him I was an East Fife supporter, he smiled and replied in that unique manner that was so familiar to anyone who had ever heard the great man speak. *"I saw them luft the cup at Hampden in thurty-eight",* he told me, before going on to describe how he had just been a young laddie at the time and had been passed over the heads of a crowd of Methil miners down to the front of the terracing so that he could see the game.

Those Saturday evening and Sunday afternoon highlights programmes were good not just for watching the goals and football skills on display; they offered an insight into what most of the Scottish First Division grounds were like at that time. They were full of character, unlike the bland all-seater stadiums of the present day, and in most cases they consisted of a grandstand along one side with terracing on the other three sides which had been constructed either from poured concrete or from railway sleepers and ash. Even the grounds of the two 'Old Firm' clubs followed the same basic layout.

Of the eighteen First Division grounds of the 1972/73 season, five no longer exist; and most of the others, with perhaps the exception of Arbroath's Gayfield, Ayr United's SomersetPark and Morton's Cappielow, are no longer recogniseable as the stadiums they once were. The five grounds that no longer exist all had a distinct character, something that is sorely missing from today's game.

Take Airdrieonians' BroomfieldPark, for example, which had an old fashioned pavilion in one corner with an ornate upper tier that seated around 100 spectators. Then there was Dumbarton's BogheadPark, which boasted the smallest main grandstand of any league ground, being just twenty-five feet in length (less than eight metres).

In addition to the televised Scottish highlights, BBC's Sportsreel also featured highlights from the main game that had been shown on England's Match of the Day that evening; and, it has to be said, from what I saw on TV, the English grounds of the early 1970's were equally full of character.

Southampton's ground at that time, The Dell, had three rather fragile looking platforms suspended over the terracing at one end, which were affectionately known as the 'Chocolate Boxes'. Then there was DerbyCounty's Baseball Ground, which started the season with a lush green playing surface that eventually became transformed into a mud bath during the winter months due to poor drainage. Wolves' ground, Molineux, boasted a cover along one side that looked for all the world like a lot of old fashioned railway platform covers joined together; and at some of the other English First Division venues, including West Ham's Boleyn Ground (often mistakenly referred to as Upton Park), the terracing behind each goal came so close to the pitch that the goal nets had to be extremely shallow. The crowd could in all probability have reached out over the advertisement hoardings and touched the goalkeeper!

As for live matches broadcast on television, all I seem to recall watching, apart from the World Cup, was the annual Scotland v England international. Of course, there was no such thing as satellite television back then; in fact most households only had two channels, BBC1 and STV. If you wanted to watch BBC2 you had to invest in a special TV aerial.

Colour television was also in its infancy in the early 1970's, and we got our first colour 'set' in 1972. I was lucky, as most of my friends didn't get a colour telly until their dads decided that it was a necessity for the World Cup in 1974. And of course, for reasons described in the previous chapter, matches shown on television were the only games that I was able to see (providing my dad didn't want to 'watch the other side'), so I suppose I had to be thankful for small mercies.

On the evening of Wednesday 20th September 1972, four days after the home defeat to Hibernian, the first leg of the League Cup second round clash with cup holders Partick Thistle got under way with a crowd of just over four thousand lining the Bayview terraces, all hoping to see the men in black and gold keep their League Cup hopes alive. They were not to be disappointed.

A goal with just eight minutes remaining from teenage centre-forward Doug Dailey, who headed home from a Billy McPhee corner, proved to be enough to separate the sides on the night and give East Fife a one-goal advantage going into the second leg.

Three days later, on Saturday 23rd September, it was back to league business and a trip to Ayrshire to face Kilmarnock at RugbyPark. Killie were having a poor start to their league campaign, and had lost all three matches played so far, with their leaky defence having conceded nine goals in the process.

Surely, I thought, East Fife would seize this golden opportunity to get their league challenge back on track? As it turned out on this occasion I was absolutely correct!

In a desperate attempt to stem their recent run of bad results, Kilmarnock had made several changes to their team, but it was to no avail. East Fife were on top right from the start, and early in the second half they were sitting on a comfortable three goal lead thanks to counters from Kevin Hegarty, Doug Dailey and Walter Borthwick. The home side eventually pulled a goal back from the penalty spot, but by that time the points were already in the bag and East Fife returned home with a three-one victory.

A week later, on Saturday 30th September, Hearts were the visitors to Bayview for the latest league match; and, as both teams were in winning form, this game promised to be a cracker!

Naturally, I was desperate to attend the match. Having previously been refused permission to go to Bayview for the Hibs game a fortnight earlier, as previously explained, I decided to take a different approach. I would ask my dad to end his 'Bayview boycott' and take me himself!

After all, his East Fife scarf was still hanging inside his bedroom wardrobe, so it must be assumed that he had kept hold of it in case he decided to make a return to the Bayview terraces after an absence of twenty years. However, I can't say that I was all that surprised at his reaction, which was practically the same as before.

EAST FIFE
WALTER BORTHWICK

EAST FIFE
INSIDE-FORWARD
KEVIN HEGGARTY

"Me tak' ye tae a fitba' match? No. Not a chance!" he informed me in no uncertain manner, before adding that phrase which I had heard him say so often; *"there's too much violence at fitba' grunds nooadays, no' like when I used tae go".*

"But lots o' ma pals go wi' their dads, so how can you no' tak' me?" I retorted. After harping on for several minutes about how unfairly I was being treated, I finally realised that I was pushing him too far when his face started to take on the colour of a Hearts jersey.

And so, with there being no amateur game to attend, I reluctantly resigned myself, once again, to an afternoon of listening to David Francey's football commentary on Radio Scotland; which, in all probability, would once again feature one half of the 'Old Firm'.

As for the Hearts match, it did turn out to be a memorable one as far as East Fife supporters were concerned, with visitors' 'keeper Kenny Garland called into action on more than one occasion during the opening stages as Billy McPhee and Kevin Hegarty came close to breaking the deadlock. At the other end, the home side had 'keeper Davie Gorman and defender Davie Clarke to thank for denying the visitors. Yes, the game had turned out to be a cracker right enough!

After more of the same during the second period, the decisive moment came mid-way through the half when teenage substitute Graham Honeyman, just two minutes after taking to the field, scored the only goal of the game. BayviewPark erupted, but unfortunately the celebrations were marred when fighting broke out between rival supporters on the covered terracing, and the police were forced to move in and restore order.

Sadly, it appeared that once again my dad had been proved correct in his assumption that football grounds were far from safe environments; a point that he was only too keen to emphasise when he learned of the incident. I was beginning to think that I might never set foot in BayviewPark!

6

After having beaten Hearts by that single Graham Honeyman goal, East Fife moved up to fifth place in the league table, just two points behind leaders Celtic, and an incredible eight places ahead of the other half of the 'Old Firm', Rangers.

It has to be said, however, that it was still early days as far as the league competition was concerned, with only five league matches having been played so far.

"That's us up to fifth", I proudly announced to one of my classmates, John, a Raith Rovers supporter, when I arrived at school on the Monday morning following the Hearts game.

"No you're not. East Fife are sixth", he retorted. *"I saw the league table in yesterday's paper".*

"Well, the Sporting Post league table quite definitely shows us in fifth place", I indignantly replied.

We both eventually decided to settle the argument by bringing the relevant newspaper cuttings to school the next day to prove the point.

"There, told you so", I proudly announced the next morning when I thrust the league table snipped from Saturday night's Sporting Post into his face. However, to my dismay, John then produced a league table cut from the Sunday People that clearly showed East Fife in sixth place, with Dundee occupying fifth spot.

The argument continued as we entered the classroom, where the teacher overheard us as we took our seats. He intervened; and, being a football fan himself, was able to come up with the answer after having studied both league tables.

"It looks like the Sunday People, which is an English newspaper, is still calculating the Scottish League tables using the old 'goal average' system, as opposed to 'goal difference', which was the method introduced in Scotland just over a year ago", he observed. *"It's the Sporting Post table that's the correct one".*

So East Fife WERE in fifth place! It was with an extremely smug expression on my face that I neatly folded the newspaper cutting and placed it back in my pocket, before gleefully reminding the Raith fan that it didn't really matter to me if East Fife were in fifth or sixth place in the First Division in any case as Raith Rovers were still languishing in the league beneath us!

On Wednesday 4th October, East Fife travelled through to Glasgow for the second leg of their League Cup second round tie against Partick Thistle at Firhill. The men from Methil were a goal ahead from the first leg, played at Bayview a fortnight earlier, and they were going to have to be at their very best if they wanted to eliminate the cup holders.

In the event, the Fife adopted defensive tactics in order to preserve their slender lead; and, although this approach to the game was not exactly to the taste of the football purists in the 5,000 crowd, it did the trick.

The closest that Thistle came to scoring was a penalty claim in the early stages of the second half when Peter McQuade appeared to handle the ball on the goal line. Fortunately for the Methil men the referee waved away the Partick protests.

After surviving intense pressure from Thistle as the match entered its latter stages, during which time the Fife defence denied the home side even one single shot on target, the final whistle eventually sounded and the men in black and gold were through to the quarter-finals!

Three days later it was back to league business, and East Fife journeyed across to West Lothian to face Falkirk, who were sitting seven places below the Methil club in the league table.

ABERDEEN
CENTRE-FORWARD
JOE HARPER

EAST FIFE
GOALKEEPER
DAVID GORMAN

Following their defensive performance against Partick Thistle, which had drawn criticism from those purists who preferred a more attacking style of play, East Fife belied their stuffy reputation by racing to a four-one half-time lead thanks to a Kevin Hegarty brace along with single counters from Doug Dailey and Graham Honeyman.

Despite scoring twice during the second half, the 'Bairns' just couldn't plough back the deficit, and the Fife ran out winners by four goals to three to maintain fifth place in the league table.

Confidence, therefore, was high for the League Cup quarter-final clash with Aberdeen, the first leg of which was played just four days after the Falkirk victory, on Wednesday 11th October at Pittodrie.

The 'Dons' went into the cup-tie on the back of a league defeat to Hearts, who East Fife had beaten just over a week earlier. However, on the same afternoon that the Fife had beaten Hearts, Aberdeen had netted seven against Motherwell. The Fife defence were going to have to be on their toes to keep the likes of Joe Harper, who had scored four against the 'Steel Men', at bay!

On the night, East Fife turned out to be no match for a rampant Aberdeen side, and a 3-0 home victory was the outcome. In fact, according to the following morning's newspaper reports, the Methil men had goalkeeper Dave Gorman to thank for preventing a complete rout! It looked very much like my dream of East Fife reaching the League Cup final for the first time since the heady days of the 1950's was all but over.

It was back to league business on Saturday 14th October and the visit of Ayr United to Bayview. The 'Honest Men' were sitting just one place below East Fife, on the same points total but with a slightly inferior goal difference, so it promised to be a close affair, and that's exactly how it turned out.

With a Bayview crowd of 4,320 looking on, Billy McPhee opened the home side's account during the first half, only for Ayr's George McLean to equalise before the interval.

AYR UNITED
GEORGE MCLEAN

AYR UNITED
INSIDE-RIGHT
JOHN GRAHAM

During the second forty-five, Johnny Graham gave the 'Honest Men' a 2-1 lead, but East Fife battled away and equalised through Mike Green to make it 2-2, which is how the game finished. It sounded like it had been an exciting match, and I was becoming increasingly frustrated that my dad would not allow me to set foot inside BayviewPark.

At school on the Monday morning, I bumped into my Raith chum, John, (he of the league position disagreement), and of course the conversation once again turned to the weekend's football.

"Why is it that you support Raith?" I decided to ask, as this question had been bothering me for some time.

"It's because my dad used to play for them", came the reply. *"That's why we go to every home game at Stark's Park. It's in his blood. I could ask him to take you as well if you like!"*

So there I was, desperate to go to an East Fife match, but was being offered the chance to go to see Raith Rovers, their local rivals. It went against my principles, but as I was getting the chance to attend a senior football match for the first time I decided to swallow my pride.

As I was to be under the supervision of John's dad, surely I couldn't come to any harm, so there was just the possibility that my dad would allow me to go. That evening, after having presented my latest case, he said he would have to think about it.

7

As I waited patiently for my dad to approve my proposed visit to Stark's Park, there was another football matter that everyone at school was talking about. On the evening of Wednesday 18th October, Scotland were due to kick off their qualification campaign for the 1974 World Cup in Germany with a match against Denmark in Copenhagen.

The Scots hadn't qualified for the finals since before I had even been born, and all I really knew about the World Cup was that England had won it in 1966; England had won it in 1966; and, England had won it in 1966.

To my pleasant surprise, it turned out that this was one of these rare occasions that a Scotland game was going to be broadcast live on television. If there wasn't anything more important for my dad to watch on the other channel, like his favourite police detective series 'Softly Softly', then there was a fair chance that I would get to see it.

In the event, dad had to go out, so I was left in peace to enjoy the game, which turned out to be an emphatic 4-1 victory for Scotland thanks to goals from Lou Macari, Jimmy Bone, Joe Harper and Willie Morgan. It was a fantastic start to the World Cup campaign; and, with only three teams in Scotland's group, the other country being Czechoslovakia, there was a good chance we could qualify for the first time since 1958!

As the end of the week approached, I decided to broach the subject of my proposed trip to Stark's Park once again.

"So, you'll be with John and his dad all the time?" enquired my father. *"Well, I suppose you'd better tell him that you're allowed to go then. Raith are in the bottom league, after all. I don't suppose there'll be much chance of trouble at that level".*

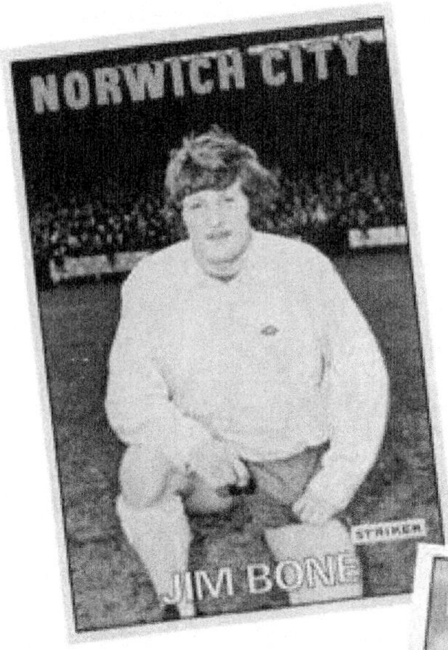
NORWICH CITY
STRIKER
JIM BONE

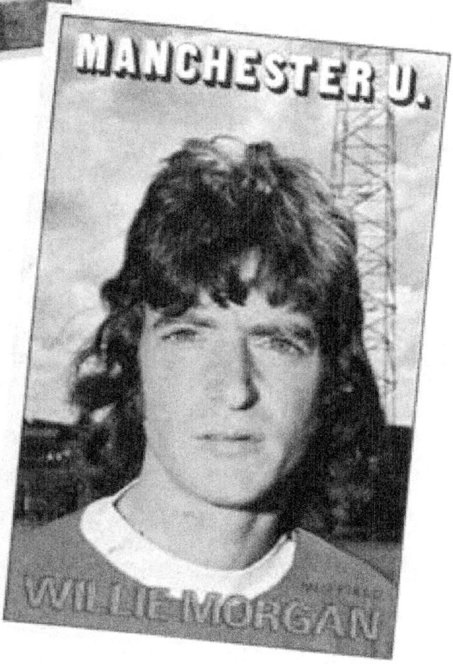
MANCHESTER U.
WILLIE MORGAN

What he had obviously failed to notice was that Raith's opponents that day were their hated local rivals Dunfermline Athletic, so there was actually a fair chance that trouble could break out on the terraces!

And so it came to pass that, on Saturday 21st October 1972, I attended my first ever senior football match, at Stark's Park in Kirkcaldy. Despite the promise that I would be kept under adult supervision throughout the entire game, however, John's dad disappeared into the pub for a couple of pre-match beers and we never saw him again until after the final whistle!

I have to say that my first impression of Raith Rovers' home ground was not great. Unlike the only other sports stadium that I had set foot in at that time, Murrayfield rugby ground (which I hasten to add I had visited on a school trip with my parents' full approval), Stark's Park looked like it had certainly seen better days.

It had a completely unorthodox layout, with a grandstand that started at the half-way line but went all the way around the south-east corner to encroach on the south terracing.

Most of the terracing consisted of railway sleepers and ash; and, in the south-west corner, where the banking rose to a considerable height, some of the sleepers had come loose and had rolled down the slope.

The central part of the south terrace was covered; and, on its corrugated iron roof, you could just make out an old faded advertisement for 'Nelson Cigarettes' that must have been there since Scottish football's halcyon days of the 1950's.

Along the west side, behind which ran the main Dundee to Edinburgh railway line, there was a narrow terrace, again constructed from sleepers and ash; the central part of which was covered by a very old small wooden enclosure that sat at a slight angle to the pitch and looked not unlike an old railway station platform cover.

At half-time, whilst queuing at the pie stall which was situated under this ancient structure, I overheard some home supporters lovingly refer to it as 'The Coo Shed', which I thought rather appropriate. The pies, I have to admit, were good, and had apparently been supplied by Pillan's, the now defunct Kirkcaldy baker.

The ground's only areas of concreted terracing were situated on a narrow area in front of the grandstand which stretched for the entire length of that side of the ground; and at the front of the north terrace, the rear of which was constructed from railway sleepers and ash and covered with a corrugated iron roof structure not dissimilar to that on the south side.

In hindsight, however, I have to admit that Stark's Park was full of character back in the early 1970's. It was a 'real' football ground, the development of which had been hindered over the years by the fact it was hemmed in by a railway line on the west side, Pratt Street and its associated tenement housing on the east side; and an almost sheer drop behind the south terrace, at the foot of which lay the Tiel Burn.

In those days, Stark's Park was totally unlike the characterless and banal football stadiums that we have become so accustomed to in the modern day. Unfortunately, the Kirkcaldy ground has now gone down the same road despite the limitations of its geographical situation, with the 'Coo Shed' and traditional terracing now but a distant memory. And Pillan's pies are no longer on sale.

I can't remember what the score was that day, nor do I care, but I have to admit that I thoroughly enjoyed the whole experience; so much so that I was now even more determined to see my first East Fife game at Bayview.

And as for my pal John's dad's football career with Raith Rovers, it later transpired that he had only ever made two appearances for the Kirkcaldy club!

8

On the same day that I attended my first ever senior football match at Stark's Park, East Fife were facing Celtic through in Glasgow in a league fixture, but unfortunately, there was to be no repeat of the result at the same venue just two months earlier when the honours had been shared. With the Glasgow side in top form as they prepared for their midweek European Cup clash with Hungarian side Ujpest Dosza, Harry Hood gave Celtic the lead on the stroke of half-time before late second half goals from Dixie Deans and Bobby Lennox sealed a three-nil victory.

A week later, on 28th October, Partick Thistle were due to visit Methil on league business. I knew that any attempt on my part to attend the match would prove fruitless, so I resigned myself to yet another Saturday watching local amateurs Anster United. However, a perusal of that weekend's amateur league fixtures in Wednesday's East Fife Mail revealed that Anster weren't playing at home; they were playing Crail Amateurs at Beech Walk Park in Crail, around five miles to the east.

At school the next day, I spoke to some of my pals who were also regulars at Anster's home games at Bankie Park, and persuaded them that it would be a good idea to catch the 'bus along to Crail that Saturday.

"It'll be just like getting the supporters' 'bus to an away game", I said in an attempt to make the adventure sound more exciting. Eventually, a few of them agreed that it might be good fun; and so, on the Saturday afternoon, we all boarded the 'bus to Crail.

I have to say we looked the part. Some of our number, myself included, were sporting red and white bar scarves. Mine had been knitted by my granny, who had also kitted me out in a matching bauble hat.

After we had made our way to the rear of the vehicle, as was the traditional thing for young teenagers to do, someone suggested we should be true football supporters and sing football songs. Before long, we were in full voice.

Of course, as well as denouncing that day's opponents, we had to give Anster's other two local rivals, Pittenweem Rovers and St Monans Swallows, a mention:

> "Oh, wur on oor way to Beech Walk,
> We shall not be moved;
> Wur on oor way to Beech Walk,
> We shall not be moved;
> No' by the Crail, Pin'weem or Siminnins,
> We shall not be moved!"

Followed by, at the tops of our voices:

> "UNITED! UNITED! UNITED! UNITED!"

It didn't take long for the conductress to get sick of it; and, as she made her way towards the back of the 'bus with her ticket machine clattering off the seats as well as some passengers' shoulders, she bellowed:

"Will you lot behave yersels an' keep the noise doon? There's fowks at the front are feart there's gaun tae be a fitba' riot!"

Of course, as was the case with everyone who lived in the close-knit fishing villages of East Neuk at that time, everybody knew everyone else, and even the local 'bus conductress knew who most of us were. Which, of course, meant that the inevitable cheeky retort from one of our party resulted in the all-too commonly heard reply:

"I ken a' yer mithers, so if ye dinnae behave yersels' ah'll hae them a' tell't, an' then ye'll a' be sorry".

This, of course, had little effect; and, still in high spirits, we disembarked in the sleepy village of Crail, which was suddenly awakened to the sound of our boisterous behaviour as we made our way to BeechWalkPark.

The football ground in Crail, from what I remember, was one of the better amateur grounds in its day. Although it was a public park, the football pitch was hemmed in by stone walls down either side, and metal railings ran the full length of the pitch for spectators to lean on. In the south-west corner, there was an old wooden pavilion that had obviously been lovingly maintained over the years, on the front of which was proudly emblazoned 'Crail Amateur Football Club'.

As kick off approached, we positioned ourselves on the opposite side of the pitch from where the meagre home 'support', most of whom were elderly gentlemen wearing 'bunnets' and long overcoats, were assembled in a small group.

When the teams emerged from the pavilion, with Anster wearing their traditional red and Crail sporting black and gold stripes not unlike the East Fife jerseys of the 1950's, we went mad and jumped up and down waving our scarves and chanting *"ANSTER! ANSTER! ANSTER!"* ... which brought inevitable glowers from the locals, who were obviously accustomed to a more tranquil atmosphere at Beech Walk on a Saturday afternoon.

After the match got under way, we were no less vociferous, and our vocal encouragement was obviously making an impact because it didn't take long for Anster to build up a commanding lead.

The team's ability, of course, had also been a contributing factor, and it has to be said that Anster United were a force to be reckoned with in local amateur football circles back in the day. One of their players had even played a trial for Raith Rovers reserves; and another, it was rumoured, had once made an appearance for Scunthorpe United!

Half time arrived; and, with there being no pie stall, we were forced to troop down to the local baker's shop in search of sustenance. Of course, at the back of three on a Saturday afternoon, there wasn't going to be much on offer in a sleepy village's only baker's shop, but to my delight I spied two pies in a small glass-fronted oven behind the counter.

First come first served!

"Can I hae a hot pie please?" I asked the lady behind the counter.

"Sorry, there's nane left" she replied.

"But there's twa' in the oven", I pointed out.

"Aye, but they're reserved" I was told. *"Ye hiv tae order hot pies if ye want wan on a Setterday. It's so as they're no' wastit".*

And so we all had to make do with a packet of crisps and a bar of chocolate.

We arrived back at the game just after the second half had started; and, from then until the final whistle, Anster's superiority was in evidence as the red and whites ran up a final tally of five goals against a solitary counter for the home side.

We were euphoric, and invaded the pitch to congratulate the team. BeechWalkPark had probably never witnessed such scenes; and, in all probability, neither had the players!

We then made our way back to the centre of the village, where the 'bus to take us home eventually pulled in. Then, as we all climbed aboard, a familiar face was staring back at us from the front seat; the same conductress who had chastised us earlier that day.

It transpired that whilst we had been at the game, the 'bus that had brought us to Crail had gone all the way to Dundee, turned around, and was now on its return journey with the same crew. We were warned, sternly, as we trooped past the 'clippie', to be on our best behaviour; and that the threat of being reported to our parents still stood. But of course, to young adolescents, that's like a red rag to a bull, and our return journey was no different to the one we had made earlier.

On arriving home just in time for the football results at five o'clock, however, I was brought back down to earth with a bump when I learned that East Fife had lost at home to Partick Thistle. The smile was well and truly wiped from my face!

9

The first match played in November 1972 was the second leg of the League Cup quarter final against Aberdeen at Bayview on the evening of Wednesday 1st November. The Fife were, unfortunately, three goals down from the first leg at Pittodrie, which had been played three weeks earlier, and nobody really expected the team to be able to turn around such a deficit.

In the event, the 'Dons' netted four against a single counter from Kevin Hegarty that evening to record a rather emphatic aggregate score of 7-1. My dreams of a return to the glory days of the late 40's and early 50's, when the men in black and gold had won the League Cup no fewer than three times, had been well and truly put to bed!

However, despite this latest loss and the recent home defeat to Partick Thistle, the East Fife supporters were still reflecting on what had been a fairly successful season so far. The club was sitting in a commendable tenth place in the eighteen-team First Division, having won four, drawn one and lost four of the ten games played to date.

"Well, at least we can now focus our attention on the league", was the general consensus of opinion at school on the morning following the League Cup exit. As naïve youngsters, we thought that a club of East Fife's calibre was more than capable of making its mark in the higher echelons of the league; but we were careful, of course, not to kid ourselves on that we could actually win the League Championship, which in all probability was destined, yet again, for one of the two 'Old Firm' clubs.

We also believed (and perhaps with some justification), that European football was not out of the question, because a final league position of fourth or fifth would mean qualification for the recently introduced UEFA Cup tournament.

The Bayview

Printed & Published by Artigraf Printing Company, Buckhaven. Price 5p.

At the second attempt Kevin manages to beat the startled Dons keeper.

SCOTTISH LEAGUE
DIVISION ONE

SATURDAY, 4th NOVEMBER, 1972
BAYVIEW PARK, METHIL.
Kick-off 3 p.m.

EAST FIFE
VERSUS
DUMBARTON

EAST FIFE FOOTBALL CLUB OFFICIAL PROGRAMME

In order to do that, of course, league points had to be won, and the visit of Dumbarton to Bayview on Saturday 4th November presented an ideal opportunity for full points to be taken from a team that was, after all, competing in the top flight of Scottish football for the first time since having been relegated in 1922!

A crowd of 4,127 looked on as the Fife took a deserved lead mid-way through the first half when a fierce drive from Billy McPhee could only be parried by Dumbarton 'keeper Laurie Williams, and Kevin Hegarty was on hand to force the ball home.

Early in the second half, Walter Borthwick set Billy McPhee up for the second goal, after which the visitors never looked like taking anything from the game despite scoring a late consolation through Tom McAdam. That victory proved to be enough to leapfrog Falkirk and claim ninth position in the league table, with the 'Bairns' having lost at home to Hearts on the same afternoon.

A week later, the Fife had the opportunity to avenge their League Cup exit to Aberdeen with a trip to Pittodrie to face the 'Dons' in a league fixture, and what a ding-dong battle it turned out to be. Going into this game, Aberdeen were sitting fourth in the league table on thirteen points, four points behind leaders Celtic and just two points ahead of ninth-placed East Fife.

The Fife started the game in lively fashion; and, mid-way through the first half, the home supporters in the 11,500 crowd were stunned into silence when a neat one-two between Billy McPhee and Kevin Hegarty resulted in McPhee blasting the ball home just inside Aberdeen 'keeper Bobby Clark's left-hand post. Further chances then followed, and it was perhaps no surprise when Graham Honeyman fired a John Bernard corner into the net on the half-hour mark to make it two-nil and send the travelling supporters into raptures.

However, the home side started the second half with all guns blazing, and just three minutes into the second period Drew Jarvie managed to reduce the deficit.

EAST FIFE
Ernie McGarr

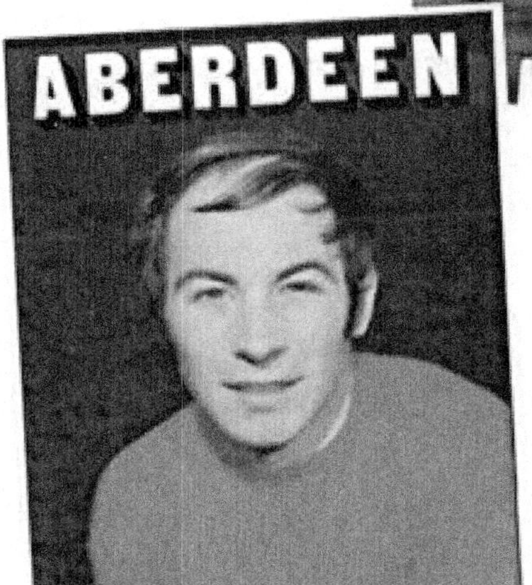
ABERDEEN
INSIDE-LEFT
DREW JARVIE

As the second half progressed, East Fife had 'keeper Ernie McGarr, who was making his debut that afternoon, to thank for denying the Dons on a number of occasions, but the home side's relentless pressure eventually paid off when Alex. Willoughby levelled the match on the hour mark.

The visitors did their best to stem the waves of Aberdeen attack, but after an own goal from Peter McQuade and a penalty from Dougie Robb made the score 4-2 in favour of the home side, it looked to be all over for the Methil men. They refused to give up, however, and some late pressure resulted in Kevin Hegarty pulling a goal back with five minutes remaining, but it was all in vain and the Dons eventually emerged victors by four goals to three.

During the following midweek, on Wednesday 15th November, Scotland were back in action for the second of their World Cup qualifying matches, this time at Hampden Park, with Denmark again the opponents. Unfortunately, this game wasn't transmitted live on television, but highlights were shown later that evening on BBC's 'Sportsreel'.

The Scots started the game in blistering fashion, and it was no surprise when Kenny Dalglish opening the scoring after just two minutes. When Peter Lorimer doubled the Scots' tally three minutes into the second half, there looked to be no way back for the Danes, and that's how the game finished despite Lorimer getting his marching orders with seven minutes of the match remaining.

Scotland were now in a commanding position at the top of their three team section, with four points from two wins and a goal difference of plus five. Denmark were as good as out of the running at this stage; and the other team, Czechoslovakia, had yet to play a game.

With the Scots being in such rampant form, I couldn't wait for the next match, against the Czechs at HampdenPark, but I was going to have a long wait as it wasn't scheduled to be played until September 1973!

The Bayview

Printed & Published by Artigraf Printing Company, Buckhaven. Price 5p.

Kevin Hegarty keeps East Fife's hopes alive as he scores their third goal against Aberdeen last Saturday.

SCOTTISH LEAGUE DIVISION ONE

SATURDAY, 18th NOVEMBER, 1972
BAYVIEW PARK, METHIL.
Kick-off 3 p.m.

EAST FIFE
VERSUS
DUNDEE UNITED

EAST FIFE FOOTBALL CLUB OFFICIAL PROGRAMME

As I have explained previously, I had yet to attend an East Fife match due to the ridiculous notion (in my eyes) of my father's that BayviewPark at this time was not a safe environment for a thirteen year old. I was so desperate to go, however, that I hatched a cunning plan in the days leading up to the next home game, against Dundee United on Saturday 18th November.

The plan was to persuade my wee brother, several years my junior, to accompany me to the game in the belief that, if we were found out, then he would be in bigger trouble than me due to his tender years, and would inevitably bear the brunt of our parents' wrath. He was initially reluctant, but eventually agreed to go after I promised to buy him a pie at the game.

And so, the pair of us boarded the 'bus from Cellardyke to Leven, from where we walked over the BawbeeBridge and up the brae to BayviewPark. I can still vividly remember standing in front of the main turnstiles in Wellesley Road, gazing up at the admission prices, which read 30 pence for adults and 15 pence for boys and old age pensioners. Transfer to the grandstand could be had once inside the ground for an additional fee.

The rattle of the turnstiles was almost deafening as we paid our money before climbing the flight of stairs at the south-west corner; from where I had my first-ever view of BayviewPark. Having only ever been at one senior football ground before this, Stark's Park, my immediate impression was one of immense pride. The neat ground that lay before me was infinitely far superior to the higgledy-piggledy Kirkcaldy ground that I had visited some weeks earlier.

Immediately to the right of my vantage point was a modern pavilion, constructed only a couple of years earlier, on top of which was situated an enclosed glass-fronted seating area for the club officials. Immediately to the east of this was the grandstand, a corrugated iron structure that had been in use for just over fifty years, having been opened not long after the club was admitted to the Scottish League in 1921.

The other three sides were neatly terraced; the terracing behind the west goal being concreted, with the other two sides constructed from railway sleepers and ash. Directly opposite the grandstand was the north terrace, the central part of which was covered by a corrugated roof.

Strangely, I can remember very little of the match itself, except for the fact that it was played on a very slippery surface, and that the players of both sides struggled to keep their feet.

Following a goal-less first half, a goal from Billy McPhee shortly after the interval sealed the points for East Fife, but I didn't see the goal as my plan to take my wee brother with me backfired at this point. He wasn't at all interested in the game, and had been amusing himself by running amongst the legs of the spectators on the packed terracing behind the goal. Of course, he managed to get himself lost; and, as I frantically searched for him, there came the most enormous roar as the ball hit the back of the net for the only goal of the game. As the crowd celebrated, I was panicking, and was having terrifying visions of having to explain what had happened to my mum and dad.

I could just picture the scene. Me standing in front of them and having to undergo the most intense interrogation with my shameful head bowed, and with a policeman taking notes as his patrol car sat outside with engine running and blue lights flashing.

"So, run this past us again. Just how, exactly, did you manage to lose your little brother in Methil?"

Fortunately, he was found, and we both managed to eventually make our way back to Cellardyke without further mishap. I don't know if the trauma of getting lost in a football crowd had anything to do with it, but my brother has never to this day set foot in another football ground!

10

As well as having a favourite Scottish team, I had a favourite English team, Liverpool, who were also the English club favoured by most of my school chums. The Anfield side were, at the time, challenging yet again for the English League Championship.

Unlike some English sides at that time, Liverpool didn't have many Scots in their squad, but that was more than made up for in that their manager was the legendary Scotsman Bill Shankly, one of the greatest football characters of all time.

We all loved his down-to-earth views on the game that he expressed during television interviews, most of which were liberally laced with his own unique brand of humour. His most well-known quote at that time was probably:

"Some people think that football is a matter of life and death. I assure you, it's much more serious than that".

Another was: *"In my time at Anfield we always said that we had the best two teams on Merseyside – Liverpool and Liverpool Reserves",* which surely even the most diehard Everton fan couldn't help but find amusing.

Then there was the interview after a match during which a player had been flagged offside when he hadn't actually been interfering with play. When asked for his opinion on the matter, Shankly's reply was simply: *"Listen son, if one of my players isn't interfering with play then I'll have him substituted".*

On the field of play, Bill Shankly had his side playing an exciting brand of football; and, when Liverpool were featured on the television highlights programmes, they were simply a joy to watch.

In my minds eye I can still see striker Kevin Keegan banging in the goals in front of a packed 'Kop', ably assisted by the likes of Emlyn Hughes, John Toshack, Steve Heighway and Scottish internationalist Peter Cormack.

Along with most of my classmates, I keenly followed Liverpool's battle for supremacy at the top of the English League, and their result was always one of the first that I looked for at five o'clock on a Saturday afternoon. But there could be no denying that in football terms East Fife mattered to me more than anything else, and confidence was undoubtedly high following the victory over Dundee United.

This feeling of confidence was emphasised a week later, on 25th November, when Motherwell were beaten by a single goal on their own soil thanks to a Billy McPhee strike which was his fourth counter in as many games.

At the beginning of December, the club was sitting in seventh place in the eighteen-team First Division; just a point behind Dundee United and two points behind both Hearts and Aberdeen. Third placed Rangers were only three points ahead and second placed Hibs were just a point clear of the Ibrox side. Even at this stage in the season, with thirteen games played, league leaders Celtic had only eight points more than East Fife!

On the second day of the month, the Methil men made the short trip north to face Dundee at Dens Park; where, with the 'Dark-Blues' breathing down East Fife's neck just a point behind in the league table, a closely-fought encounter was anticipated. Unfortunately, that's not how the game turned out.

Although the first forty-five minutes were evenly balanced, with the game goal-less at the interval, a quick-fire double from Dundee's John Duncan mid-way through the second half put the Dens men well in control. East Fife huffed and puffed and tried desperately to claw their way back into the game, but it was all in vain, and two late counters from Gordon Wallace and Jocky Scott inside the final ten minutes sealed a four-nil victory for the home side.

DUNDEE
Gordon Wallace
OUTSIDE RIGHT

DUNDEE
INSIDE-LEFT
JOHN SCOTT

That result saw Dundee leap-frog East Fife into seventh place; but the Methil men only slipped down one place in the league table because Ayr United, who had also been just a point behind the Fife, were beaten by St. Johnstone at Muirton.

On the following Saturday, 9th December, East Fife had a great chance to make amends for their heavy defeat at Dens with the visit of lowly Airdrieonians to Bayview. The 'Diamonds' had not been having a good season so far, and were sitting second bottom of the league on six points, equal with bottom club Kilmarnock, but with a slightly superior goal difference.

After having attended my first ever East Fife match three weeks earlier against Dundee United, I was desperate to take in another game; and, after having given the venture some considerable thought, decided that I would risk going along to Methil without my little brother, who had proved to be nothing more than a liability during my previous visit to Bayview.

I boarded the 13:30 'bus from Cellardyke bound for Leven that Saturday afternoon, and was delighted to find that one of my school chums, a fellow East Fife supporter, was already seated on the 'bus and bound for Bayview.

After having managed to convince the 'bus conductress that I was just thirteen and therefore still eligible for a child fare (full fare was payable from age fourteen in the early 1970's!), I settled into my seat and excitedly chatted to my pal about what the game was going to be like and who would bag the goals in what was surely going to be a one-sided encounter. We were playing a 'diddy' team from the bottom of the league after all!

As the 'bus trundled west through the East Neuk villages, my pal pulled a folded up East Fife team photo from his pocket, which he had cut from the then popular 'Goal' football magazine.

Gazing at the picture, we worked our way along the front and back rows of players, naming each one and discussing their qualities.

East Fife team photos were prized possessions back then. Never in my wildest dreams did I think that one day, many years into the future, I would be club photographer and would be responsible for taking the official East Fife team photo at the beginning of each season!

Eventually we arrived at the Shorehead in Leven, from where we made our way over the BawbeeBridge along with groups of other black and gold bedecked supporters, all heading for Bayview.

Once inside the ground, we took up position behind the west goal as we waited for the game to begin. The official attendance of 3,239 was about a thousand less than the previous home game against Dundee United, but there were still enough supporters lining the terraces to create a good atmosphere.

East Fife won the toss, and elected to play towards the east goal, so we joined the throngs of home supporters who were starting to make their way around to the other end as the game got under way, such was the tradition before the installation of segregation fences limited movement within many football grounds, including Bayview.

During the early stages of the game, there was no doubt which team was going to win. East Fife were attacking Airdrie from all angles, completely belying their reputation as a defensive side, and it was no surprise when Kevin Hegarty broke the deadlock after eighteen minutes.

Then, mid-way through the first half, East Fife were awarded a free-kick thirty yards from goal; and it was at this point that I saw, for the first time, the power of Billy McPhee's much-revered left foot. The inside-left was a master of the dead ball situation; and, when a direct free-kick was awarded within sight of goal, it was actually as good as being awarded a penalty, such was the accuracy and ferocity of Billy's powerful shot.

The Bayview

Printed & Published by Artigraf Printing Company, Buckhaven. Price 5p.

Allan brilliantly saves a McPhee free-kick.

SCOTTISH LEAGUE
DIVISION ONE

SATURDAY, 9th DECEMBER, 1972
BAYVIEW PARK, METHIL.
Kick-off 3 p.m.

EAST FIFE
VERSUS
AIRDRIE

EAST FIFE FOOTBALL CLUB OFFICIAL PROGRAMME

"Watch this, the ball is as good as in the back of the net when Billy takes a free kick", my pal assured me; and, sure enough, the East Fife man duly fired the ball into the top corner, leaving the diving Airdrie 'keeper clawing at thin air. Anyone who blinked at that moment would have missed the goal, such was the speed at which the ball had been powered through the air.

The interval arrived with the score at two-nil in favour of the Fife; and, as we made our way back around to the 'Bayview Bar' end for the second half, the discussion was very much centred around how many goals we were going to net that afternoon.

With darkness falling and the Bayview floodlights now illuminating the action, East Fife resumed the second half in the same fashion that they had ended the first, and soon had the visitors' goal under pressure. That pressure finally paid off when, midway through the half, Billy McPhee unleashed an unstoppable shot from all of thirty yards that gave the Airdrie 'keeper no chance. I can still quite clearly recall the ball becoming firmly wedged behind one of the net stanchions, such was the power of the shot!

A decisive three-nil victory was the outcome, and as soon as the final whistle sounded we ran out of the exit gate and along Wellesley Road, down the brae and over the Bawbee Bridge, before arriving out of breath at the Shorehead just in time to catch the five o'clock 'bus back up the coast.

After the 'bus had pulled away from the Shorehead, the conductress slowly made her way around the passengers, collecting the fares and issuing tickets. When she reached me, I fumbled in my pocket for the fare, and realised that I was a penny short. This meant that I could only buy a ticket as far as Anstruther, but it didn't really matter because it only meant that I would have to walk an extra half-mile or so.

However, as the 'bus made its way up the coast, I hatched a cunning plan; a plan which, with the use of local knowledge, should enable me to disembark at my usual stop, Burnside Terrace.

When the 'bus arrived in Anstruther, I put my plan into action and stayed on board. Then, when the Burnside Terrace stop came into view a few minutes later, I stood up and made for the exit. As expected, when the vehicle was coming to a standstill, I felt a sharp tap on my shoulder from the conductress.

"You only bocht a ticket tae Anster", she told me in no uncertain terms. *"Yer noo in Cellardyke."*

"No I'm not, this is still Anster", I replied.

"Burnside Terrace is a Cellardyke stop", the conductress informed me with a condescending air of superiority. *"You'll hae tae pay a single fare frae Anster tae Cellardyke"*.

"But the boundary between Anstruther and Cellardyke is Caddies Burn, which used to follow the course of this street, hence the name Burnside Terrace. The burn is now piped underground, but it's still the boundary. The 'bus stop on this side of the road is in Anster, although it's true to say that the stop on the other side of the road is in Cellardyke".

"The laddie's richt, ye ken", said an elderly bunnet-wearing gentleman sitting nearby. *"Strictly speakin' this is still Anster"*.

And so, the conductress had no other option but to admit defeat; and it was with a smug look on my face that I disembarked and made my way home, where my parents had not the slightest suspicion regarding my whereabouts that afternoon. I made up my mind there and then that I was going to make the Saturday afternoon trip to Methil a regular occurrence.

That evening's Sporting Post made for enjoyable reading. East Fife had maintained eighth place in the league table, and were now on equal points with seventh-placed Dundee, who had only managed to draw with Falkirk.

Second-placed Hibs were sitting only four points in front of East Fife; and, although leaders Celtic were a further four points ahead, it seemed to this misguided but euphoric young teenager that a push for the Scottish League Championship might just be possible after all!

11

Going into the final weeks of 1972, following their three-nil victory over Airdrieonians, East Fife were in a favourable position as far as their league campaign was concerned. Unfortunately, this 'feel good factor', was about to change rather quickly.

On Saturday 16th December the Methil men travelled to Perth to face St. Johnstone at MuirtonPark. With the Saints sitting five points and three places behind East Fife, confidence was high that at least a point could be taken from the match, but unfortunately things didn't go quite to plan.

When the half-time interval arrived, the home side were in a commanding position following two goals from Henry Hall; his first from the penalty spot.

After Kevin Hegarty had reduced the deficit on the hour mark, it seemed for a brief period that East Fife might be in with a chance of taking something from the game, but the travelling supporters' hopes were dashed just two minutes later when Jim Pearson restored the home team's two goal advantage.

Then, in 73 minutes, Billy McPhee raised hopes in the black and gold ranks once again when he netted from the penalty spot. Unfortunately, it turned out to be a case of déjà vu, because just three minutes later Pearson netted again to make it 4-2 for the Perth side, and that's how the match finished.

Suddenly I wasn't so confident about our challenge for a final league position amongst the elite come the end of the season, but fortunately East Fife's position of eighth place was maintained thanks to nearest challengers Ayr United getting thumped by an incredible eight goals to one by Hibs at Easter Road on the same afternoon.

On the following Friday, my spirits and those of my class mates were high as the school Christmas holidays got under way. The talk at school all week, however, had been more about Rangers' forthcoming visit to Bayview rather than the imminent Christmas festivities.

And so, on the day after the school holidays commenced, the so-called Rangers supporters who attended school with me joined the East Fife supporters on the 'bus to Leven on Saturday 23rd December in order to make their once-a-season visit to a Rangers game, and their demeaning attitude towards the regular supporters of a 'wee team' like East Fife was positively aggravating.

We were outnumbered, naturally, by these 'armchair experts', and had no other option but to sit quietly and absorb the negative comments, although deep inside we were quietly confident that East Fife were more than capable of making a game of it. Rangers were, after all, just four points in front - and we had home advantage!

Sadly, in the event, the Fife were like rabbits caught in the headlights as Rangers ramped up an unassailable four-goal lead before half-time through a Derek Johnstone brace and single counters from Quinton Young and Derek Parlane.

Although it pains me to admit it, Rangers appeared to take their foot off the pedal during the second half; seemingly content to sit back on their four-goal advantage and see the game out. There was no further scoring.

I didn't wait for the final whistle, however, because in order to avoid the taunts of the Rangers supporters on the way home, I left the game early and caught the half past four 'bus back to Cellardyke. Fortunately, I still had Christmas to look forward to, and it would be another fortnight before I had to face up to the torments of the Ibrox 'faithful' on my return to school.

As I sat alone with my thoughts on the 'bus back to Cellardyke, I had the opportunity to reflect on the game I had just witnessed.

One factor that my eternally optimistic mind had failed to consider, of course, whilst confidently predicting a favourable outcome earlier that afternoon, was that Rangers were at the time European Cup Winners Cup holders, having won the trophy by defeating Moscow Dynamo by three goals to two in Barcelona just a matter of months earlier.

The fact that they were a formidable side at the time cannot be disputed. In fact, the Rangers team that played at Bayview that afternoon contained no fewer than nine of the players who had tasted European success at the Nou Camp. And although I didn't really want to admit it, I had actually enjoyed watching household names that I had seen so often on television; players like Peter McCloy, Tommy McLean, and John Greig; all displaying their football skills right in front of my eyes.

Of course, I couldn't help but be familiar with the Rangers players, or the Celtic players for that matter, because the 'Old Firm' were always the preferred choice when the television companies were deciding which games to cover for the weekly highlights programmes.

As the 'bus slowly made its way east towards Cellardyke, I reflected on various aspects of the match I had watched that afternoon, but there was one particular incident that intrigued me. During the half-time interval, a huge cheer suddenly emanated from the Rangers supporters (who had taken total possession of the covered terracing on the north side of Bayview) when the scores were being put up on the half-time scoreboard (a necessity in the days long before the advent of the mobile 'phone).

It transpired that the wild scenes of jubilant celebration, which were even more intense than their goal celebrations had been during the first half, were because the scoreboard indicated that Hibs were one-nil up against Celtic at Parkhead. Now, maybe it was because I had led a reasonably sheltered life in the East Neuk of Fife, where sectarianism was almost unheard of, but I simply couldn't understand why one team's misfortune should give another team's supporters cause for such unadulterated joy.

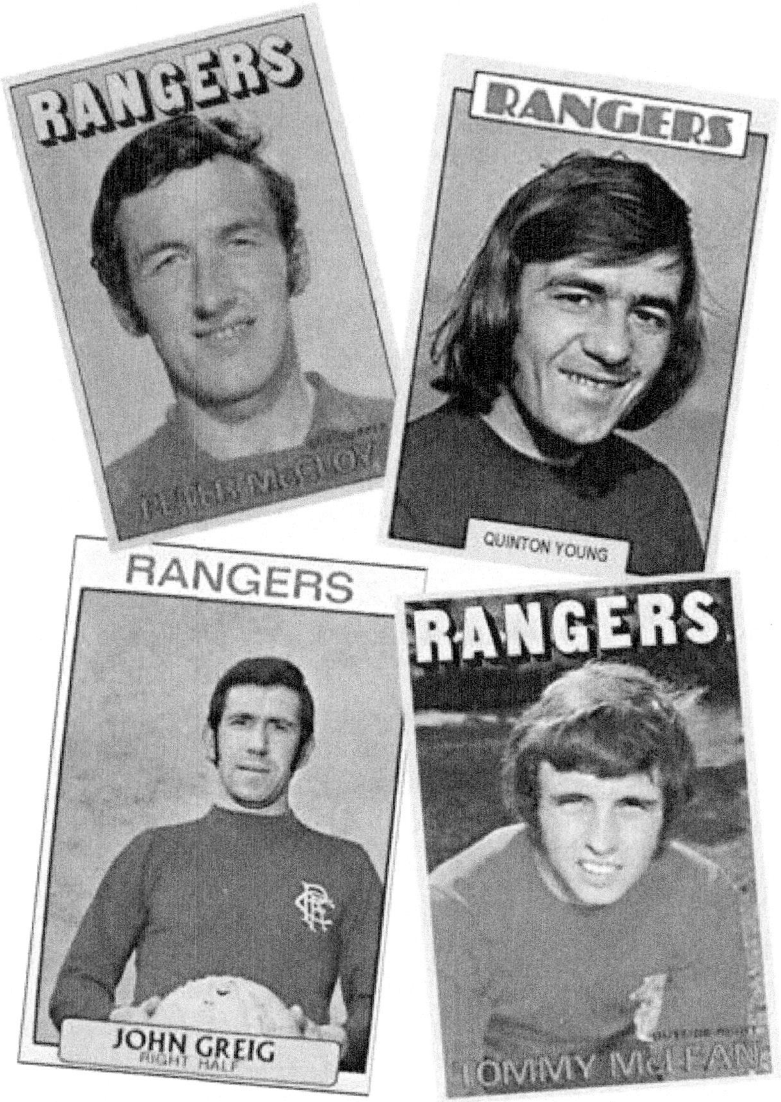
RANGERS
RANGERS
QUINTON YOUNG
RANGERS
JOHN GREIG
RIGHT HALF
RANGERS

I found the whole thing rather puzzling at the time; and, even in the present day, despite being older and wiser and having a better understanding of such matters, I still don't fully understand how so-called football supporters can hold such an obsession. If that's what supporting one of the 'Old Firm' clubs is all about, then I'll stick to supporting my 'wee team', thank you very much.

A couple of days later, on Christmas morning, the disappointment of the Rangers result had faded somewhat, and I was delighted to see that my previous correspondence to the fat man in the red suit with the big jolly face had been honoured in the shape of a leather football. It had always been my dream to own one, and surely I would now be the envy of my pals!

Unfortunately, closer inspection revealed that this ball was the same one that had been on display for some considerable time in the window of a back-street ironmonger's shop in Anstruther; a shop which for some unknown reason seemed to specialise in goods not normally stocked within such an establishment.

The ball was probably of the same type that East Fife had been accustomed to playing with during their halcyon years; and, unlike most footballs of the early 1970's, it consisted of a rubber bladder placed inside a leather-panelled sphere. The hole through which the bladder had been inserted was laced up, and I found that heading the ball could be a painful experience if my head made contact with the lacing.

Through time, the polished leather surface became badly scuffed, before the glossy shine eventually disappeared altogether. This resulted in the ball being covered with a porous surface that became easily saturated on wet grass, which made it heavy and difficult to control, and which also made heading an even more painful experience!

However, I had to be grateful that, in the true spirit of Christmas, my dad had momentarily cast aside his hatred of football and had honoured my request for such an item.

But that wasn't all. As well as the football, I received a cassette recorder, a gadget that was all the rage at the time. And what made it even better was that this cassette recorder was different from most, as it was one of the first to have a radio incorporated within the device, which meant that I would now be able to record all of my favourite music directly from the radio on to a cassette tape.

Another huge benefit was that, in future, I would be able to listen to football broadcasts on Saturday afternoons from the comfort of my bedroom, if I wasn't at an East Fife game. In addition to this, I would be able to take my new radio cassette with me when watching Anster United at BankiePark, which would enable me to keep up to date with football developments elsewhere. Maybe life wasn't so bad after all.

It didn't take long for the joys of Christmas to fade, however, and during the days that followed I started to think about East Fife's next match, away to Greenock Morton on the second last day of the year.

The Fife couldn't possibly lose three in a row. Or could they?

12

It was now the middle of winter, and for the past couple of months it had become increasingly difficult to climb out of bed at just after six in the morning before trudging all the way to Anstruther and all the way back delivering newspapers and magazines. One very slight consolation was that every Wednesday was East Fife Mail day, when the Leven-based local newspaper was delivered. The paper always carried an extended report from Saturday's East Fife game, and more often than not a picture was included in the report.

As I said though, this was only a very slight consolation, because the East Fife Mail in those days was a rather large and heavy broadsheet publication, and on Wednesday mornings my green canvas paper sack was backbreaking to lift, never mind carry along the street.

Almost every single house on my round had a 'Mail' delivered; and, with the added weight of around forty Dundee Couriers and a number of Daily Expresses and Daily Records thrown in, I had to stop for several rests before I had even reached the first customer's house. And all this for the measly reward of eighty pence per week!

Some customers, especially the RAF officers who lived in the big MOD houses on East Forth Street, had English newspapers delivered. These arrived at the shop separately from the Scottish papers in a little van, which was quite often late. On these occasions I had to go at some rate if I wanted to finish my round in time for school, which incidentally involved a further walk of around two miles from my house. Looking back, I am surprised that I managed to stay awake at school after having risen not long after six in the morning and walked over four miles before eventually sitting down in the classroom.

EAST FIFE
RIGHT-HALF
BOBBY CAIRNS

EAST FIFE
OUTSIDE-LEFT
BILLY McPHEE

It was currently the school holidays, however. I didn't have to rise so early in the morning for my paper round, and I could even go back to bed once it was finished, if I so desired.

The end of the year was now fast approaching, and the football season was almost at the half-way stage. East Fife's league form to date had been far better that that of the previous campaign, when they had been sitting second bottom of the table as the end of the year approached; and, although recent defeats may have dented my confidence a little, I was still sure that the Fife were capable of finishing the season near the top of the table.

As I stated earlier, I was even of the opinion that we were capable of attaining a final league position in the top four or five; a scenario that would bring European football to Methil! Of course, being only thirteen years old at the time, I was more than a little naïve, and didn't fully appreciate the fact that it was highly unlikely a part-time provincial side like East Fife could maintain a serious challenge amongst the country's elite, as the bigger clubs obviously had a much larger pool of players to call on during the latter stages of the season when injuries started to take their toll.

East Fife's final game of 1972, exactly a week after their four-nil home defeat to Rangers, was a trip to face Greenock Morton at Cappielow on Saturday 30th December. I was brimful of confidence on the eve of the match, as I was positive the team couldn't possibly run up a 'hat-trick' of successive defeats. Going into this fixture, Morton were sitting thirteenth in the table; four places and four points behind the Methil men; and had, like East Fife, lost heavily on their previous outing. The Fife were due a win, so surely Morton were there for the taking?

Once again, however, the game did not go according to plan; and, after only five minutes' play, the home side took the lead through their Danish centre-forward Gert Christensen. When Billy Armstrong doubled Morton's advantage, the outcome didn't look good for the men in black and gold; and when Don Gillies added a third midway through the second period it was all but over for the Fife.

Although Billy McPhee eventually managed to pull a goal back, there was no further scoring and the match ended in a convincing win for the Greenock side.

Just two days later, on New Year's Day 1973, Arbroath made the short journey south to Methil. Having lost three league games in a row, morale at Bayview was understandably not as high as it could have been; and the home supporters in the crowd of just under 5,000 were no doubt hopeful that the East Fife players had abstained from the 'demon drink' during their New Year celebrations and had gone to bed just after the bells!

When the game kicked off, however, both sides looked sluggish and tired, and a rather dull game ensued. Despite having scored five against Falkirk just two days earlier, Arbroath looked shot-shy, and it was East Fife who created most of the first-half chances, during which Kevin Hegarty, Billy McPhee and Walter Borthwick all coming close to breaking the deadlock.

The rather drab fare continued after the interval, with chances few and far between. Then, midway through the second half, the game suddenly sparked into life when Arbroath's Ernie Winchester handled in the penalty area and the referee pointed to the spot. Billy McPhee took the resulting kick and placed the ball neatly into the bottom right-hand corner of the net to put the Fife a goal ahead. Or so they thought.

As the players congratulated the scorer, the referee decided to spoil the party by deciding that the kick had to be re-taken because one of the East Fife players had strayed into the box. Up stepped Billy McPhee once again; and once again he placed the ball perfectly into the bottom right-hand corner. This time it was decreed that there had been no infringement, and the home side were in front.

The Methil men now had their tails up, and peppered the Arbroath goal during the final twenty minutes. Their pressure finally paid off five minutes before the end when Jim Hamilton netted number two with a scorching drive, and the points were safe!

EAST FIFE
E.F.F.C.
JIMMY HAMILTON

EAST FIFE
E.F.F.C.
CENTRE-HALF
JOHN MARTIS

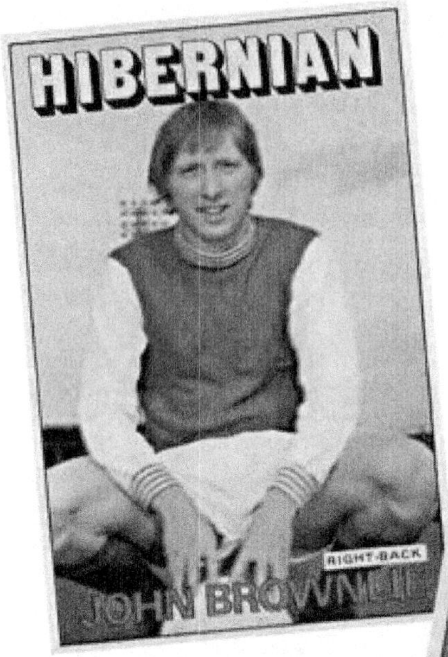
HIBERNIAN
RIGHT-BACK
JOHN BROWNLIE

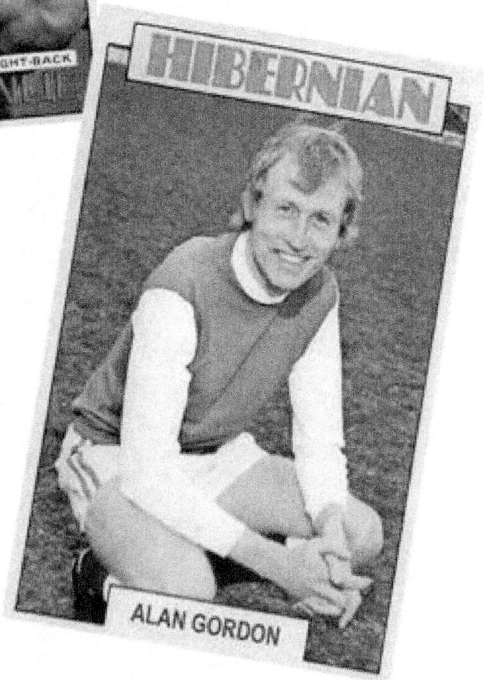
HIBERNIAN
ALAN GORDON

East Fife climbed up two places in the league table to eighth thanks to this victory, and the doom and gloom that had surrounded the club since their last win, at the beginning of December, was all but lifted.

Five days later, the Methil men travelled through to Edinburgh to face league leaders Hibs, who had claimed pole position following a seven-nil thumping of city rivals Hearts at Easter Road on New Year's Day. There could be no doubt that East Fife had a tough task ahead of them, and they were going to have to be at their very best to take anything from the match.

With recently appointed Scotland manager Willie Ormond looking on from the grandstand, East Fife surprised the 15,000 crowd by taking the game to the league leaders during the opening exchanges. Playing down the famous Easter Road slope, the Methil men harried the table-toppers right from the start, and for the first twenty minutes it was home custodian Jim Herriot who was the busier 'keeper. Indeed, had he not pulled off a magnificent save from a Billy McPhee pile-driver, the Fife would have been ahead at half-time.

Unfortunately, just before the interval, Hibs' Scottish international full back John Brownlie was carried off after colliding with East Fife's Ian Printy, and was subsequently taken to hospital with a broken leg.

As his players were to play up the energy-sapping Easter Road slope during the second half, East Fife Manager Pat Quinn decided that the best way to keep the Hibs 'goal machine' at bay was to pack the defence; and this approach to the game, although not popular with many spectators, almost paid off.

The league leaders mounted wave after wave of attack during the second forty-five, and it took until the eighty-eighth minute before they finally broke the deadlock through centre-forward Alan Gordon.

Having come so close to denying the league leaders, defeat was a bitter pill to swallow for the travelling supporters; but the men in black and gold could hold their heads high.

They had, after all, conceded only one goal compared to the seven conceded by Hearts at the same venue just a week earlier!

As was normally the case when East Fife were playing away from home, I had spent the afternoon watching Anster United at Bankie Park, and was able to keep updated with developments at Easter Road thanks to having my new radio cassette pressed to my ear.

Needless to say, as the 'Old Firm' Derby was also taking place that afternoon, updates from Edinburgh were few and far between, and John Brownlie's broken leg seemed to be the only thing that was deemed worthy of reporting from East Fife's visit to Easter Road.

That evening, however, the Sporting Post gave a good report on East Fife's heroic display against Hibs, which more than whetted my appetite for the next home game, against Kilmarnock on the following Saturday. I couldn't wait!

13

Although the first two matches played in 1973 had resulted in one win and one defeat, the overall mood at BayviewPark was positive following the encouraging performance against league leaders Hibernian at Easter Road.

On Saturday 13th January, I made my first 'bus journey of the new year from Cellardyke along to Leven, from where I walked with the other black and gold clad supporters making their way over the Bawbee Bridge and up the hill to Bayview Park. It had been several weeks since my last visit, for the Rangers match in mid-December; and, despite East Fife having suffered a heavy defeat that afternoon, there was a spring in my step. Today's opponents were Kilmarnock, who were languishing at the foot of the table, and I was confident that we would take full points from the Ayrshire side.

After the match got under way, with East Fife kicking towards the Aberhill end, my pre-match confidence was justified when Billy McPhee opened the scoring during the early stages from the penalty spot after Killie centre-half Alan Lee had handled a Kevin Hegarty chip inside the box. The Methil men kept the visitors' goal under siege as the game progressed, with chances at the other end of the park few and far between.

Although the Fife were only a goal to the good as I joined the home supporters on their migration from one end of the ground to the other, I was confident that more goals would surely come during the second half. Darkness had now descended, and the beam from the floodlights was illuminating the scene before me as I leaned on a crush barrier and munched my half-time pie. Although it had now turned cold and there was a light drizzle falling, at that moment there was nowhere else in the world I would rather be.

That nostalgic moment in time that has remained with me through all the years that I have followed East Fife, and what wouldn't I give to be transported back in time to BayviewPark on a Saturday afternoon in the early 1970's!

When the second half got under way, East Fife resumed where they had left off; and, ten minutes into the second period, Walter Borthwick neatly headed over the advancing Kilmarnock goalkeeper to double the home advantage. Eventually, the result was put beyond doubt when Graham Honeyman fired home through a crowd of defenders following a goalmouth melee to make the final score three-nil.

After the final whistles had blown all around Scotland that afternoon, the East Fife supporters eagerly awaited the results from elsewhere, hoping to hear that Ayr United had dropped at least a point to Arbroath. With the 'Honest Men' sitting just a point ahead but with an inferior goal difference, there was a good chance that the Fife had leap-frogged Ayr into eighth place. Unfortunately, Ayr had beaten the 'Red Lichties' two-nil, so it was a case of 'as you were' as far as league positions were concerned.

We were still in ninth place, though, and had widened the gap over St. Johnstone to three points, as the Perth side had only managed to share the spoils with Motherwell.

On the following Saturday, 20th January, East Fife journeyed over to Edinburgh once again, this time to face Hearts at Tynecastle. With the maroons having been thumped seven-nil by Hibernian just a few weeks earlier, and with East Fife having then almost forced a draw with Hibs, I was confident that the men in black and gold were more than capable of taking something from the match.

Of course, there was no way I could be at the game, and had no other option but to keep myself informed of the game's progress through listening to the updates on Radio Scotland through the medium of my radio cassette from the sanctuary of my bedroom.

When the half-time score came through as nil-nil, my belief that we could at least win a share of the spoils with Hearts seemed to be justified, and I proceeded to sit on my bed with my ear almost glued to the radio waiting for updates from Tynecastle as the afternoon progressed.

As that day's matches got closer and closer to reaching their conclusions, it seemed like a no-scoring draw might be on the cards. Then, to my horror, news came through that Hearts had taken the lead through Eddie Thomson with just five minutes left on the clock. It looked very much like there was going to be a repeat of East Fife's last visit to Edinburgh, just a fortnight earlier, when Hibs had netted a late winner.

I angrily switched off the radio and lay back on my bed, before turning over and punching my fist into the pillow. After mulling over how cruel this game of football could be for several minutes, I decided to go downstairs and switch on the television to watch the football results coming through on the BBC 'Grandstand' teleprinter. When the result came through that Ayr United had lost at home to Celtic, my mood was lifted a little with the knowledge that the 'Honest Men' would still be just a point ahead of East Fife in the table. Eventually, the result from Tynecastle came through:

Heart of Midlothian . . . . . . 1 . . . . East Fife 1

YES!!! We must have netted a late equaliser!

I leapt up off the couch and punched the air. It looked very much like East Fife had been a match for Hearts after all, and I eagerly awaited the regional football reports that always followed the results service, which were usually read out by Alastair Alexander, a legendary Scottish television presenter who was in the same league as the previously mentioned television legends David Francey and Bob Crampsey.

Alastair Alexander's reports on the Scottish matches were always delivered in an amusing manner, where he would incorporate a play on words in order to maintain the viewer's attention.

However, there was nothing amusing about his report on the Hearts versus East Fife match, which he described as being about as one-sided as a game could be. East Fife's goal, he said, came from the only chance created by the Methil side all afternoon. Surely this couldn't possibly be correct. Was the presenter actually a Hearts supporter whose nose had been put out of joint thanks to that late equaliser?

I couldn't wait to read the report in that evening's Sporting Post, which would surely paint a very different picture of the game. And so, at seven o'clock, I set out on my customary two-mile round trip from Cellardyke to Anstruther to buy my copy.

Unfortunately, the newspaper's match report didn't make for pleasant reading, and completely backed up what I had heard earlier on television. East Fife had been under the cosh for almost the entire game, and had played for eighty-five minutes, until Hearts scored, with just one forward and ten defenders!

From all accounts it was only after the home side had taken the lead that East Fife manager Pat Quinn decided to replace left-back Ian Printy with wing-half Drew Noble and instruct his players to go looking for the equaliser. And that move paid off almost immediately when Graham Honeyman capitalised on a Walter Borthwick shot that had rebounded off Hearts' 'keeper Garland to fire the ball home.

However, when all is said and done, the final result is infinitely more important than the performance on the day. The final score of one goal apiece was there for all to see in back and white on the front page of my Saturday evening sports paper.

What was most pleasing, though, was the fact that East Fife still held the upper hand over Hearts in the four meetings there had been between the sides since the Fife had returned to the top flight, with one victory recorded over the Edinburgh side along with three draws.

And we were now sitting eighth in the league table!

14

On 27th January 1973, a week after having ground out that gruelling one-all draw with Hearts at Tynecastle, East Fife had a home league fixture against Falkirk.

Going into this match, the Methil men were eighth in the league table, having leapfrogged Ayr United thanks to that late equaliser in Edinburgh. Falkirk were languishing seven places below; and, with the visitors having been thumped three-nil from Partick Thistle in their previous outing, it looked very much like form was in favour of the home side.

Unfortunately, I was short of funds on this particular Saturday, having blown my entire paper round money (and other savings) on David Bowie's *'The Rise and Fall of Ziggy Stardust and the Spiders From Mars'*, which had just gone to the top of the UK album chart. It was an album every young teenager simply had to have at that time, even if it meant missing a home game at Bayview!

That afternoon, at four o'clock, I switched on my radio and tuned in to Radio Scotland to see what the featured game was, and was delighted to find that the BBC radio crew were at BayviewPark for the second half of the East Fife v Falkirk match!

With the legendary David Francey at the microphone, I listened eagerly as the second half got under way, and the unorthodox and unpredictable Francey settled into his commentary with the following observation:

"Ah-hah! I see a gentleman sitting a few rows in front of me fiddling with the buttons on his transistor radio. No doubt he's tuning in to this afternoon's commentary and wondering what game we're covering today".

"The game's coming from BayviewPark, sir, and I am sitting just a few rows behind you! Ah-hah – the gentleman has realised that it's him I am talking to and has just turned around and given me a wave. Good afternoon to you, sir, enjoy the game!"

The East Fife supporters, naturally, had been expecting a comfortable home victory over the 'Bairns', but that's not how it turned out. The game had been only six minutes old when right-back Bobby Duncan uncharacteristically headed the ball past 'keeper Davie Gorman into his own net to give Falkirk an early lead; then, ten minutes later, the visitors had almost doubled their advantage when Alex. Ferguson, the future Aberdeen and Manchester United manager, just failed to connect with the goal at his mercy.

Despite having created good chances as the first half progressed, the Methil men just couldn't find the net; and, when Falkirk netted their second on the stroke of half-time it looked very much like it wasn't going to be East Fife's day.

Just five minutes after the live radio broadcast had commenced at the beginning of the second half, the feelings of doom and gloom were exacerbated when the home side were denied what looked like a certain penalty after Graham Honeyman had clearly been impeded inside the box. From my vantage point, sitting on my bed with the volume of my radio up to full blast, it had looked like (in my mind's eye) a 'stone-waller', and I vented my frustration vociferously.

All that my cries and wails achieved, however, was a shout upstairs from my mum asking if I could please stop torturing my little brother, if that's where the noise was coming from. After having reassured her that I was actually alone in the room, and that I was listening to my radio cassette, she asked that I turn the volume down to a reasonable level. And could I please stop singing so loudly along with whatever music I was playing.

I toyed with the idea of going downstairs to explain the current situation at BayviewPark, and that my raised voice was perfectly justified under the circumstances, but thought better of it.

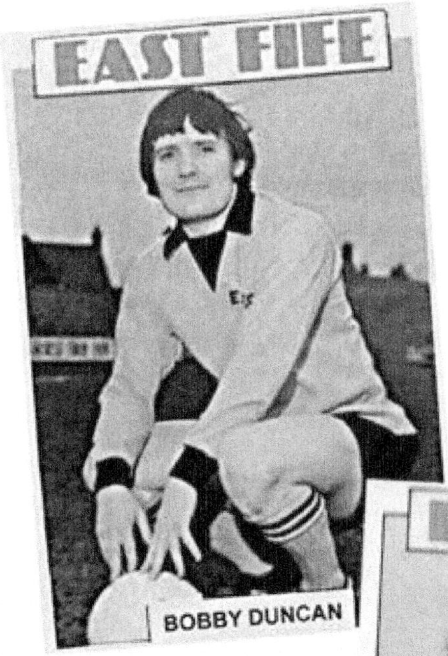
EAST FIFE
BOBBY DUNCAN

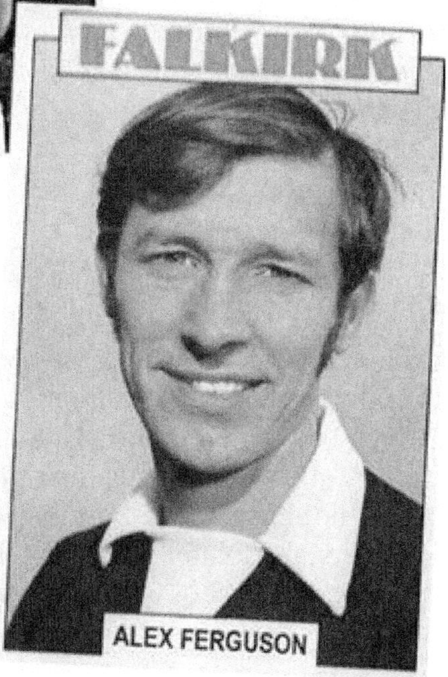
FALKIRK
ALEX FERGUSON

I lay back down on my bed and listened to the rest of the match, but from the tone of David Francey's commentary it seemed very much like a defeat for East Fife was on the cards. Eventually, with ten minutes remaining, Doug Dailey pulled a goal back, but it proved to be too little too late as far as the Methil men were concerned, and Falkirk emerged victorious by two goals to one.

A week later, on 3rd February, all thoughts of winning league points were put aside when East Fife travelled through to Glasgow to face Celtic in the Scottish Cup. The 'Hoops' were, at the time, sitting second top of the league; two points behind leaders Rangers but with three games in hand. A week earlier, the Celts had surprisingly lost to bottom club Airdrieonians; and, as one would expect, East Fife could well be on the receiving end of a backlash!

As there was no Anster United match for me to attend that afternoon, I resorted to one of my other favourite forms of Saturday entertainment when I couldn't watch football, which was watching that afternoon's live televised Rugby League match on BBC's 'Grandstand'. As well as being a football fan, I was also a bit of a rugby fan, as that was the sport that I played at school. We pupils actually had no choice in this matter if we wanted to participate in a team sport, because the WaidAcademy didn't have any football teams at that time.

Although the Rugby League game was different to the Rugby Union that we played at school, I still found it entertaining, although I have to admit that I found the different rules a little puzzling. One of the things that I found appealing about Rugby League, though, was that in those days all of the clubs were from the industrial north of England, and the players were a hardy down-to-earth sort of breed who weren't averse to the odd pitch brawl!

The Rugby League grounds that I remember from the television coverage were all very much like the typical Scottish football grounds at that time; in most cases consisting of a grandstand on one side with terracing around the other three. There were no all-seat stadiums then, and no artificial playing surfaces.

During the winter months, the playing surfaces of most of the rugby league grounds degenerated into mud baths; and, as the game wore on, it became increasingly difficult to tell one team's players from the other's, as they were all coated from head to foot in mud.

Another thing that was different in the 1970's was that the names of the Rugby League clubs didn't have the annoying suffixes that they have today; like 'Rhinos', 'Bulls', 'Tigers' or 'Warriors'. Back then it was just good old-fashioned names like Bradford Northern and Wakefield Trinity!

One of the most entertaining aspects of the live Rugby League television coverage, however, was the commentary from the legendary Eddie Waring, whose quotes and sayings in his north of England accent were a joy to listen to.

"Ee's gone for an early bath", Eddie would chortle when a muddy player was sent off following a brawl. Or *"it's an up 'n' under"* when the ball was punted high in the air. On one occasion, whilst covering a match in Hull on a cold winter's afternoon, I can remember him remarking *"eeeh, it's a full coat colder on the east coast".*

My main concern on this particular afternoon, however, was how East Fife had fared in Glasgow, and when the BBC teleprinter finally spat out the result it was perhaps no surprise that Celtic had recorded a convincing four-one victory thanks to braces from Kenny Dalglish and Dixie Deans. East Fife's only goal was scored by Billy McPhee, which I later learned whilst reading a match report had been his fiftieth for the club.

A week later, East Fife made the long journey to SomersetPark to face Ayr United in what promised to be a very tight game. The 'Honest Men' were sitting eighth in the league table after having exchanged places with East Fife once again when they beat Partick Thistle on the same afternoon that the Methil men had lost at home to Falkirk. No doubt both sides would be looking to take something from the match.

As expected, the match turned out to be evenly balanced, but it was Ayr who broke the deadlock mid-way through the first half through Rikki Fleming before Johnny Graham added a second just minutes later to give the home side a two-goal advantage.

In the second half, East Fife forced their way back into the game, and ten minutes after the restart Kevin Hegarty pulled a goal back from the penalty spot. The patience of the travelling supporters in the 4,698 crowd was eventually rewarded when Doug Dailey equalised with twenty minutes of the match to go. Unfortunately, East Fife's hopes of taking something from the game were quashed when George McLean netted a late winner for Ayr.

But despite having failed to gain any points from their most recent two league matches; and despite having failed to record a victory of any kind since their three-nil victory over Kilmarnock a month earlier, East Fife were still in the top half of the league table, albeit by a whisker.

Closer perusal of the table, however, revealed that the three clubs sitting immediately below the Methil men; St. Johnstone, Motherwell and Falkirk; all had games in hand, and all were more than capable of catching East Fife if they could turn these matches into points.

I was simply going to have to pull out all the stops in an effort to make it to the next home game, against Celtic, where I was confident that my vociferous support wouldn't be lost in what was sure to be a huge crowd, and that my assistance in this way would surely help get the team back on track!

15

On Saturday 17th February 1973, Celtic visited Methil on league business. It was a day that I had been looking forward to for some considerable time; and I was sure that, if the team could reproduce some of the form shown earlier in the season, then the boys in black and gold could well avenge the Scottish Cup defeat suffered at the hands of the 'Hoops' in Glasgow just a fortnight earlier.

The day dawned bright and sunny, although somewhat chilly, and as I watched the football preview on BBC's 'Grandstand' at lunch time I learned that several Scottish matches had been postponed following snow falls and a severe overnight frost in certain parts of the country.

To my relief, Bayview Park was one of only three First Division grounds to be declared playable that afternoon; the others being Pittodrie, where Aberdeen were due to face Ayr United; and Cappielow Park in Greenock, where Morton had St. Johnstone as visitors.

With the Methil men enjoying their best season since the club's 'Halcyon Days' of the 1950's; and with second-placed Celtic looking to take over from Rangers at the top of the table if victory could be secured that afternoon, I was certain that there could now be no reason for the television cameras to snub an East Fife home game yet again.

Since top league football had returned to Methil at the beginning of the 1971/72 season, over eighteen months earlier, neither STV's 'Scotsport' or BBC's 'Sportsreel' had featured highlights of matches from Bayview Park, despite some very important games having been played there since East Fife's promotion back to the top-flight.

The Bayview

Printed & Published by Artigraf Printing Company, Buckhaven. Price 5p.

"50 up" Billy McPhee scores his 50th goal since joining East Fife but this was not enough to keep the Fifers in the cup when they went 4 – 1 down to Celtic.

SCOTTISH LEAGUE
FIRST DIVISION

SATURDAY, FEBRUARY, 17th 1973.

Kick-off: 3 p.m.

EAST FIFE
VERSUS
CELTIC

EAST FIFE FOOTBALL CLUB OFFICIAL PROGRAMME

Surely, with only three First Division games taking place that day, and with pole position at stake, East Fife v Celtic had to be the pick of the bunch!

As usual, I boarded the No.355 'bus from Cellardyke bound for Leven at half-past-one, after having told my dad, who was still flatly refusing to allow me to go to football matches at Bayview, that I was going to St. Monans to visit my pal Donald.

Now, with just fifteen minutes to go before kick-off, I was inside the ground watching both sides go through their warm-up schedule. And Donald, who I was supposed to be visiting in St. Monans, was standing beside me!

As for the expected television coverage, however, there was no sign of a camera anywhere inside the ground; and I hadn't noticed any outside broadcast vehicles in the streets surrounding BayviewPark. Yes, it was evident that East Fife had been snubbed yet again by 'Scotsport' and 'Sportsreel'.

I should point out here and now that I am not, and never have been, a Celtic fan; far from it! But there was something thrilling about watching household names such as Bobby Murdoch, Billy McNeill, Jimmy Johnstone and Bobby Lennox go through their paces still looking good after their European Cup success five years before. And there, just a few feet in front of me as I leaned on the advertisement hoardings, was none other than a very youthful Kenny Dalglish, willingly signing autographs for his young female admirers. It was all a bit surreal!

Bayview was now filling up nicely, and a good atmosphere was building. When kick-off time eventually arrived at three o'clock, there was an 'official attendance' of 11,577 paying spectators lining the terraces, but to me the ground looked fit to burst; and I have to say that I was a little surprised on the following day when I read the crowd figure published. If BayviewPark had regularly held crowds of well over twenty thousand in the late 1940's and early 1950's, then just exactly where had they squeezed in the additional ten thousand or so spectators?

Having entered by the turnstiles at the AberhillSchool end of Bayview, Donald and I decided to remain at that end when the match got under way, as this was the goal that East Fife normally elected to play towards during the first half. To our dismay, however, they lost the toss and were forced to shoot towards the west goal for the opening forty-five minutes.

With such a large crowd in attendance, it was going to be extremely difficult to force our way round to the other end, so we just decided to stay put and give what vocal encouragement we could to goalkeeper Ernie McGarr.

The visitors started well; and, had it not been for a series of good saves from Ernie, Celtic could well have taken a commanding lead during the early stages. Now, it is highly unlikely that the East Fife 'keeper would have been able to hear me, or would have even listened if he was within earshot, but I was utterly convinced that his performance so far was entirely down to my vocal encouragement. Oh, the naïvety of a thirteen year old!

After having weathered the visitors' promising start, the Methil men slowly came into the game, and when half-time arrived the team could be reasonably satisfied with their performance so far, despite having gone behind to a goal from John 'Dixie' Deans mid-way through the half.

At least I was going to be behind the goal that my favourites were shooting towards during the second half; and, by the time the game restarted, Donald and I had been joined by a fair number of our school chums, who during the interval had somehow managed to force their way from the other end of the ground through the packed terraces.

East Fife started the second half in blistering fashion, and the game had only just got under way when Kevin Hegarty was brought down on the edge of the penalty area. The home fans bayed for a penalty; then waited with baited breath whilst the referee made his way over to where the offence had been committed to ascertain if it had occurred inside the penalty box.

CELTIC
CENTRE-HAL
BILLY McNEILL

CELTIC
CENTRE-FORWARD
JOHN DEANS

CELTIC
RIGHT-HALF
BOBBY MURDOCH

When the official turned, blew his whistle and pointed to the spot, scenes of jubilation broke out amongst us youngsters standing immediately behind the goal, as we knew that Billy McPhee rarely missed from a spot-kick. We were not to be disappointed, and BayviewPark erupted as Billy duly blasted the ball home to put the Fife level!

But there was more to follow. The cheers had hardly died down before even greater scenes of jubilation ensued when Walter Borthwick shot home past the outstretched arms of Celtic 'keeper Ally Hunter to put East Fife ahead.

Gold bedecked supporters hugged each other and schoolboys (including yours truly!) leapt over the hoardings to dance around on the park. East Fife had taken the lead against the mighty Glasgow Celtic; but would it last?

The visitors piled on the pressure with wave upon wave of attack as the game progressed; and, midway through the second half, Kenny Dalglish was sent clean through on goal. Just when it looked like an equaliser was on the cards, the striker hesitated and his weak shot was saved on the line by the hand of defender Bobby Duncan.

Bobby Murdoch stepped up to take the resulting penalty kick, only to send the ball high over the bar, to the resounding cheers of the Fife faithful. To our dismay, however, looking on from the other end of the ground, the referee decided that some East Fife players had strayed into the penalty area before the kick had been taken, and ordered a retake.

This time, Ernie McGarr saved with his foot from Harry Hood to maintain the Fifers' lead, and the scenes of ecstatic joy resumed amongst us youngsters at the Aberhill end.

Celtic continued to pressurise the home goal during the latter stages; then, with time running out, Davie Clarke was adjudged to have brought Deans down inside the box. Once again the referee pointed to the spot, and the home supporters could hardly bear to watch as Dalglish stepped up to take his side's third penalty.

Once again, however, home 'keeper McGarr was equal to the task and saved the spot-kick, sparking further great scenes of jubilation amongst the home support, and the feeling was growing amongst us that we were going to hold out for a famous victory. With two minutes to go, however, Dixie Deans broke our hearts when he squeezed a header just inside McGarr's right-hand post to square the match at two goals apiece.

When the final whistle finally went, it was a mightily relieved Celtic support that streamed out of the ground, most with smiles on their faces despite the fact that their team had failed to leapfrog Rangers and go top of the table.

The home support on the other hand, although a little disappointed that victory had been snatched from their grasp, made their way home delighted to have witnessed such a spectacle. For many, including the author, it was, and still is, one of the best football matches they had ever seen; a view backed up by Sunday Post reporter Jack Harkness, who commented:

"From the entertainment point of view, I have seen plenty of exciting games in my time, but few which excelled this one."

The result prompted questions about Celtic's ability to retain the Scottish League title, which they had held for the previous seven seasons. *"Is Celtic's seven year monopoly of the league championship at an end? Are Rangers about to win the flag after looking like also-rans? Will Hibs stymie the Old Firm and lift the title themselves?"* mused Sunday Post columnist Bill McFarlane, in his weekly 'Post Script' article.

If this was the reaction of the press after the reigning champions had dropped a point, one can only wonder what their reaction would have been if Deans hadn't bagged that late equaliser!

Fortunately, there were no instances of violence reported either before or after the match at Bayview, but the same cannot be said of a Scottish Junior Cup tie between Dundee Osborne and Ayrshire side Kilbirnie Ladeside which had been played at East EndPark in Dundee on that same afternoon.

As the match was nearing its conclusion with Osborne defending a narrow lead, one of the Kilbirnie players decided to have a swing on one of the crossbars, which snapped under his weight.

The player in question was booked, which prompted fans of the visiting club to invade the pitch in order to remonstrate with the referee. The supporters and officials of the home side were equally incensed at the wanton damage to their crossbar, and swarmed on to the pitch to remonstrate with the player who had sparked off the incident. The match was consequently held up for several minutes whilst the pitch was cleared and repairs were made.

The game was eventually restarted and played to a finish, but when the final whistle blew fighting broke out once again in front of the dressing rooms. The police were called and several squad cars raced to the scene, before order was eventually restored with the use of batons. As a result, five fans spent the rest of the weekend in the police cells.

The referee, who had once again been threatened by the visiting supporters as he made his way from the field to the pavilion after the final whistle, had to be given a police escort when he eventually left the ground to make his way home.

"It would appear that football violence isn't just confined to the Scottish League clubs", my dad observed on the following morning whilst reading a newspaper report on the incident. *"It looks like it's not safe for you to attend football matches at any level now!"*

I shudder to think what his reaction would have been if he'd found out where I was that same Saturday afternoon!

16

I was still buzzing with excitement after getting home from the Celtic game; and, as it was the best football match that I had ever witnessed, I was hungry for more. It was extremely disappointing, therefore, to discover whilst studying the following week's fixtures in that Saturday evening's Sporting Post that the fourth round of the Scottish Cup was scheduled for the following week, 24th February. As East Fife had been knocked out of the competition in the previous round, there was no game for me to attend, unless I wanted to watch the reserves take on their Aberdeen counterparts in Methil.

At school on the Monday morning, however, I discovered that there were still schoolboy tickets and seats on the 'bus available for Saturday's school trip to the Scotland v Ireland rugby international at Murrayfield, and duly put my name down.

My dad, who as previously stated forbade me from attending East Fife matches due to his belief that outbreaks of violence were commonplace at Bayview at this time, had absolutely no problem whatsoever with me going on school trips to watch Scotland at Murrayfield, as he thought that I would be supervised at all times by the teachers. What he obviously failed to realise, though, was that we were given a couple of hours' free time in the city centre before the match, during which we got up to all sorts of mischief.

Almost as soon as we got off the 'bus we would make for the joke shop in Cockburn Street to buy stink bombs, which would subsequently be let off in one of the big Princes Street stores. Another prank carried out on one occasion by one of my chums was to drop a small rubber 'Superball' off the top of the ScottMonument to see how high it would bounce. Thank God it didn't hit anyone!

For the record, Scotland beat Ireland 19-14 that afternoon, but much as I enjoyed the game I would rather have been watching East Fife. As it turned out, I was going to have to wait for some considerable time before I got another chance to hand over my fifteen pence at the Bayview turnstiles, because the next three league fixtures were all away from home; against Partick Thistle, Dumbarton and Dundee United.

Sandwiched in between the Partick and Dumbarton games there was to be a friendly against Danish side AC Horsens at Bayview, but there was no way I would be able to get along to Methil on a Wednesday evening and home again at a reasonable hour using public transport. However, it was around this time that an incident occurred which was to completely cut off my income; and, as a result, I wouldn't have been able to fund trips to Bayview Park on a Saturday afternoon in any case.

When I turned up for my paper round one cold morning, there was a bill board outside the shop stating that the rail workers were to go on strike. There was a lot of discontent amongst the country's workforce at that time, who felt that their wages weren't keeping up with inflation, which was sitting at 8% and increasing rapidly. This got us paper boys thinking.

I had been delivering papers for just over a year, and my weekly wage had remained unchanged at eighty pence during that time. I asked one of the older boys if he could remember when he last had an increase, and it turned out that his pay had remained exactly the same in all the time he had worked there; and he had started before decimal currency had been introduced two years earlier. His pay had been sixteen shillings then, the pre-decimal equivalent of eighty pence!

That evening, I decided to ask my dad what his thoughts were on the matter. He told me that when he had worked for the same newsagent during the war, about thirty years earlier, he had been paid ten shillings per week, which equated to exactly fifty pence in decimal currency. This meant that, taking inflation during the intervening years into account, our wage should now be well over £2 per week!

Dad also told me that newspapers back then weren't nearly as big as the editions that I had to deliver; in fact they only consisted of a couple of folded sheets, whereas the daily national papers of the early seventies averaged about thirty pages. And, just to make the unjustifiable situation even worse, he claimed that his round hadn't been nearly as far to walk round!

The following morning, I told my fellow paper boys what my dad had said, and we decided to take action. One of the older lads was delegated to be our spokesman, and he went through to the back shop to put our case forward to the proprietor, with the rest of us following timidly behind. We asked for a wage of £1 per week, a rise of 20p, but we weren't prepared for his reaction.

"What do you mean you want more pay? I'm making little enough as it is without you lot demanding a ridiculous wage rise that's more than double the rate of inflation! Go on, get out of it. If you're not happy, then you know what to do!"

He obviously thought we'd want to keep our jobs, but I decided to call his bluff. I continued to work until pay day; then, on my way to school after having finished my round that morning, I made a detour by the paper shop, opened the door, and threw my paper delivery sack inside.

That action rendered me unemployed, which meant that I was going to have to find some other source of income before East Fife's next home game. That was several weeks away though, and surely I could find a new job during that time, even if it meant working for another newsagent or maybe even having to get up much earlier to deliver milk!

On Saturday 3rd March 1973, East Fife journeyed through to Glasgow to face Partick Thistle at Firhill in the first of the three aforementioned back-to-back away league fixtures; and, after having given Celtic a fright at Bayview a fortnight earlier, I fully expected them to take something from this match. The 'Jags' were, after all, sitting five places below East Fife in the league table; and had a poor home record, having only won three league games at Firhill all season.

PARTICK THISTLE
JOHN GIBSON

PARTICK THISTLE
ALAN ROUGH
GOALKEEPER

The game didn't start well for the visitors, however, because after only three minutes' play future East Fife player Johnny Gibson put Partick ahead with a fifteen yard lob that gave 'keeper Ernie McGarr no chance.

That early setback only served to spark the Methil men into action; and for the remainder of the first half they put goalkeeper Alan Rough, Scotland's first choice custodian at that time, under severe pressure, but when the half-time interval arrived the 'Jags' still held their slender advantage.

It was more of the same after the interval, as East Fife remained in control of the match. Even defenders Davie Clarke and Bobby Duncan pressed forward as the half progressed, with the latter also managing to test Rough in the home goal. Eventually, with time running out, Kevin Hegarty finally netted a deserved equaliser five minutes before the end of the game, and that's how it finished.

The Fife maintained their position of ninth place in the league table thanks to this result, and even managed to narrow the gap on eighth placed Hearts to two points thanks to the Edinburgh side having lost to Arbroath at Gayfield by the eyebrow-raising score of three goals to nil.

Four days later, on Wednesday 7th March, East Fife played host to AC Horsens at Bayview in the aforementioned friendly, where a brace from Billy McPhee along with single counters from Kevin Hegarty and Doug Dailey recorded a somewhat convincing 4-0 win over the Danes.

On the following Saturday, 10th March, the Methil men were on their travels again, to face Dumbarton at Boghead; a quirky old-fashioned football ground that had been the 'Sons' home for almost a century; and was hosting top-flight football for the first time in fifty years.

Going into this game, Dumbarton were sitting second bottom of the table on just fourteen points from twenty-five games played, and were in considerable danger of making an immediate return to the Second Division.

It was no surprise, then, when the home side threw everything but the kitchen sink at East Fife right from the start!

Fortunately for East Fife, luck seemed to have deserted Dumbarton on the day, and their best chances of the game were squandered when striker Ross Mathie blasted over the bar with 'keeper McGarr on the ground; and when Davie Clarke cleared a seemingly net-bound effort off the goal-line.

The match eventually ended goal-less, and East Fife remained in ninth place thanks to a point they scarcely deserved, coupled with Motherwell's home defeat to Ayr United. Breathing down their necks in tenth place just a point behind were Morton, who had thumped Airdrie four-nil.

Off the field of play, the day was marred by violent scenes in Dundee prior to Celtic's league match at Tannadice, when hordes of visiting supporters ran amok in the Hilltown area. Several shop windows were smashed, shops were looted, and scuffles broke out with locals. There were similar scenes following the match, both in the Hilltown and in Dundee city centre.

The following morning, my dad was in his element as he read aloud the report on the incident which appeared on the front page of the Sunday Post, before concluding that this was exactly the reason that I wasn't allowed to go to football matches. If only he had known the truth!

Whilst East Fife had been battling for league points away from home, however, there had been some very welcome news regarding my employment status. When I had been passing the Fisheries Museum in Anstruther on my way home from school one afternoon I decided to go in and ask if they had any part-time jobs going, as one of my friends had managed to get a job there during the previous school summer holidays.

I was shown through to the curator's office; where, to my delight, I was offered a part-time summer job because visitor numbers were expected to start picking during the coming weeks.

My job involved performing various menial tasks, like helping to set up displays or assisting in the museum shop. I was expected to work initially on Sunday afternoons until it got busier, after which I would have to work Saturdays and Sundays. There would be no more early morning rises and no more having to walk for miles carrying a heavy newspaper delivery sack for a pittance of a reward from an unappreciative employer!

Surprisingly, the wage for working one afternoon at the museum was about the same as I had been getting paid for delivering newspapers six days a week; which meant that during the summer, when I would be working on both Saturdays and Sundays, I was going to be rich!

Working at the museum turned out to be really enjoyable; more so because our family had long been associated with the fishing industry; a tradition that was only broken when my dad opted to pursue a land-based career rather than endure the dangerous occupation that his forefathers had followed for as far back as anyone could trace.

My great-grandfather had been the owner and skipper of a steam herring drifter, and I had always wondered what life must have been like for him and for his crew, which also included other family members. The displays, photographs and other memorabilia at the museum went a long way towards giving me an appreciation of what my predecessors had to endure as part of their everyday lives.

The best part of my new job, however, was being on duty in the aquarium, where the knowledge gained from many years of playing in rock pools on the seashore at Cellardyke proved to be invaluable. I was able to tell visitors the names of all the fish in the various tanks, and on one occasion I was delighted to have a sizeable tip pressed into my hand from an appreciative American tourist!

Fortunately, Saturdays were still free for me to attend football matches, at least for the time being, but it was now three weeks since I had been to an East Fife game.

I was having severe withdrawal symptoms by now, but to make matters worse it was to be another three weeks before the next home Saturday game, against Motherwell on 31st March.

Yes, there was to be a league match against Aberdeen at Bayview on the Tuesday before the Motherwell fixture, but of course there was no way that I could get to Methil and back at a reasonable hour, especially on a 'school night'.

Drastic action was going to have to be taken, and taken soon. After having received my first wage from the museum, I once again had the means to finance trips to the football, and I wondered if it might be possible to take the No. 355 'bus to Dundee for the forthcoming game against Dundee United at Tannadice?

I knew the 'bus went to Dundee, because that was what was displayed on the destination board of the service that took me home to Cellardyke on Saturday afternoons after I had been at Bayview. During the days that followed, I started to plan my latest adventure.

17

East Fife were now entering the latter stages of their second season back in the top flight of the Scottish Football League, and there had been some notable results over the course of the season. The team had, however, built up a reputation for playing a stuffy, defensive style of football during this time, especially when playing away from home or facing the teams sitting higher up the league table.

This style of play was perhaps not to the liking of the fans who enjoyed fast attacking football, but it had contributed to the club's commendable league position as the final games of the season loomed; and, going into their league game against Dundee United at Tannadice on Saturday 24th March 1973, East Fife were sitting in a comfortable ninth place in the eighteen-team First Division table.

It was now well over a month since I had last attended an East Fife match, and in order to satisfy my craving I decided to go ahead with my plan to take the No. 355 from Cellardyke to Dundee for the game. I boarded the 'bus at one o'clock; and, after having enjoyed the scenic journey around the east coast, through Crail, Kingsbarns, St. Andrews and Tayport, I arrived at Dundee's Seagate 'bus station just after two o'clock, from where I made my way in the general direction of the floodlights that I had spotted whilst crossing the Tay Bridge. They hadn't looked to be that far from the City centre and I was sure that the walk wouldn't pose much of a problem for a reasonably fit thirteen-year-old.

What I hadn't reckoned on, however, was the steepness of the Hilltown, which is the thoroughfare that connects the centre of Dundee with the area where the two football grounds, Dens and Tannadice, are located.

Eventually, when the climb started to level out, I found myself facing the gable end of a building that proudly proclaimed:

'Wallace's Land o' Cakes, Pies and Bridies'

Great! A baker's shop! As I had had to leave home earlier than usual, there had been no time for lunch, and I was famished. A pie should put that right!

The bell on the shop door tinkled as I entered, and once inside there was a vast array of all the kinds of pies, bridies and cakes that you could dream of. Staring in my general direction from behind the counter was a young girl, not much older than myself, who was obviously a Saturday assistant.

"Could I have a pie please", I politely enquired. The girl continued to stare at me, then opened her mouth. *"Eh?"*

"A pie please", I repeated, but the girl just kept staring, then again just said *"Eh?"*

I decided the best way forward was to point at the desired delicacy.

"Ye mean a PEH?" she uttered, with a glance that implied I was the stupid one. *"Whit kind oh peh? Plenn, Ingin, Steck, Bean an Tattie? Hoat ur Cald?"*

Having been born and brought up in Cellardyke, where there's no such thing as a local dialect (or so I naïvely thought at that time), I was puzzled. Here I was, just twenty-odd miles to the north of my home town, and it appeared that they spoke a foreign language. In order to avoid further confusion, I simply replied *"the first kind you said, hot please, and could I have a can of orange to go with it?"*

"That'll be twuntee fehv pee". Fortunately, there was a price list displayed on the rear wall, so I was able to translate the cost of my lunch to twenty-five pence before bidding the young lady farewell. Munching my pie and slurping my can of juice, I continued up Hilltown, then branched off down Mains Road, from where I could see the first of the two football grounds.

It was possible to see inside this stadium from my vantage point, and the frontage of the grandstand was visible. I immediately recognized the stand to be that of Dundee's DensPark, having seen it several times on 'Scotsport' and 'Sportsreel'. The floodlights that lay just beyond this ground, therefore, had to be Tannadice, so I continued to walk in that direction. I eventually arrived at my destination and entered through the boys' gate before climbing to the top of a steep staircase, from where I surveyed the scene before me.

TannadicePark was a neat enclosure, although its modern grandstand, similar to that at Raith Rovers' Stark's Park, only stretched as far as the half-way line. The rest of the ground was terraced, with the only cover being behind the west goal. The uncovered terracing on the side opposite the grandstand was extremely high and steep, and it was here that I found an empty crush barrier to lean on.

The opening exchanges of the match were fairly even, during which both East Fife and United came close to breaking the deadlock. It was the Fife who eventually opened the scoring, however, when Billy McPhee netted from the penalty spot after Kevin Hegarty had been fouled in the box.

In order to preserve their slender lead, East Fife employed their trademark defensive tactics during the second half, and it almost paid off, but in the final minute of the game Tommy Traynor netted for the 'Tangerines' to earn the home side a share of the spoils. I didn't see the equaliser, though, because in order to catch the 'bus home at a reasonable time I was already half-way down the Hilltown!

I caught the 'bus at Seagate 'bus station, and settled back in my seat for the journey back around the eastern coast of Fife. When we reached St. Andrews, around half an hour later, a group of four elderly people clad in various items of tartan clothing boarded the 'bus and took the seats directly behind me. I could tell even before they opened their mouths that they were American tourists.

EAST FIFE

BILLY McPHEE
INSIDE FORWARD

DUNDEE UNITED

TOM TRAYNOR
OUTSIDE FORWARD

All the way from St. Andrews to Crail they drawled on and on about how much they had loved their visit to the home of golf, and about how they just loved Scotland, and the whisky, and how they were going to have to try haggis before they went back to the States.

It was starting to get on my nerves, but when the 'bus started to head out of Crail in the direction of Cellardyke, they suddenly fell silent as the vista of the Forth estuary fell before their eyes. However, the silence didn't last for long.

"Gee, will you look at that! Aint that just GORGEOUS?"

It was the same view that I had looked out on from my bedroom window for as long as I could remember, so I was used to it; but I have to admit that on this particular occasion the May Island, the Bass Rock, and the East Lothian coast and hills beyond were looking particularly radiant in the early evening sun.

I felt a tap on my shoulder.

"Hey, kid, what's the name of that island out there?" asked the gentleman sitting behind me.

"That's the MayIsland", I replied.

"Aint it just so pretty!" remarked the lady sitting next to him.

"We just love your country" she enthused. "We're living in a hotel in Edinboro, near the ScotchMonument, and we've been taking in Saint Andrews today. Bought ourselves some plaid to take back home to the States, d'ya like it?" she said as she proudly pointed towards her rather loud red tartan scarf.

I decided to take the opportunity to demonstrate my local knowledge by telling the couple that the enormous eminence a little further up the firth was the Bass Rock. I also pointed out Berwick Law, and in front of it the seaside town of North Berwick.

"Gee, is that so. And what about that little island I can just see just a little further away?" the gentleman asked, pointing into the distance.

He had me stumped. I had no idea what the name of this distant island was.

"Dinnae ken" I replied.

"Din - nae - ken" he repeated slowly. *"Gee, is that Scotch?"*

"Aye, I suppose it is" I said, after having successfully resisted the urge to point out that Scotch was actually the name given to the alcoholic beverage they had previously been enthusing about and was not the name given to the Scots dialect.

The gentleman turned around to face the other American couple sitting behind.

"Hey, the kid's teaching me to speak Scotch. How about that!"

"Gee, that's swell, what did he teach you?" they asked.

"Din-nae-ken", he replied. *"The kid says it's the name of that tiny island way up there!"*

18

Three days after my Dundee adventure, on Tuesday 27th March, East Fife hosted Aberdeen in what was their first home league game since mid-February. Of course, being unable to get myself along to Methil for midweek matches, it was a game I was going to have to miss.

I was disappointed at being unable to go, because the Aberdeen team at that time included Scotland 'keeper Bobby Clark as well as a number of household names like Arthur Graham, Willie Young, and Hungarian internationalist Zoltan Varga; who had also, incidentally, won a football gold medal at the 1964 Tokyo Olympics!

I was delighted, therefore, whilst walking home from school on the day preceding the match, to be met with a surreal scene in Anstruther's BankiePark. The entire Aberdeen squad, who were staying at a local hotel for a couple of nights either side of the game, were being put through their paces by the Dons' coaching staff, whose number included the legendary former East Fife player and manager Jimmy Bonthrone. I stood and watched, enthralled, for several minutes.

The match itself turned out to be a closely fought affair, with both Ian Printy and Johnny Love coming close for the Methil men during the first half. It was the 'Dons', however, who eventually broke the deadlock when Arthur Graham robbed East Fife right-half Jim Hamilton before sending a low cross into the danger zone, where Zoltan Varga was on hand to side-foot the ball home from close range. Try as they might, East Fife just couldn't find that all-important equaliser after the interval despite creating several chances, and in the end that Varga goal was all that separated the sides when the final whistle blew.

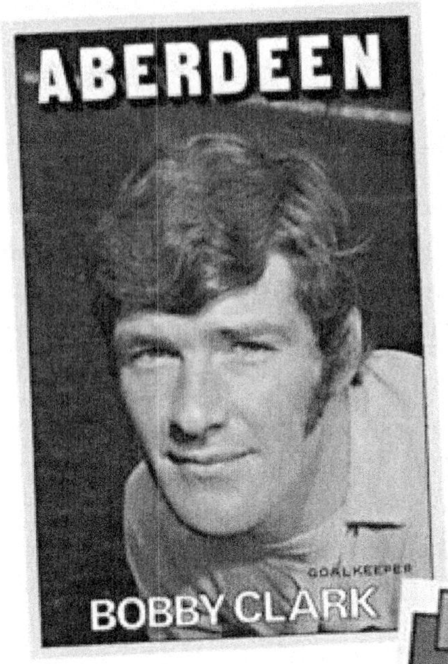
ABERDEEN
GOALKEEPER
BOBBY CLARK

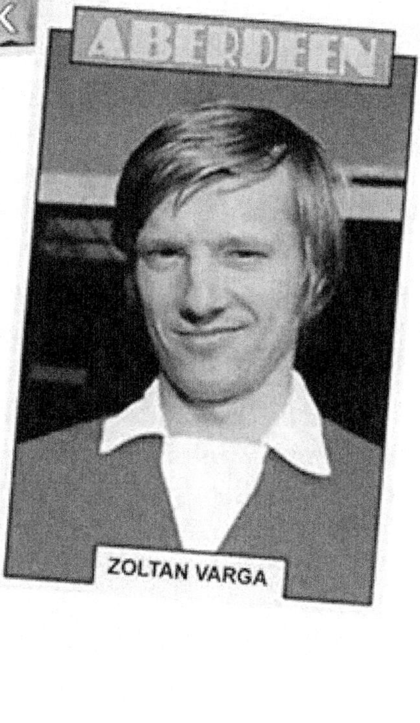
ABERDEEN
ZOLTAN VARGA

Victory at Bayview was enough to push the Dons up to fourth in the league table, but it didn't affect East Fife's standing. They were still sitting ninth in the eighteen-team First Division; twenty-one points adrift of league leaders Rangers, but thirteen points clear of bottom side Airdrieonians and ten points ahead of second bottom Kilmarnock.

With there being no end of season play-offs in those days, the teams finishing in the bottom two positions in the league table would be relegated at the end of the campaign. East Fife and all but one of the teams below them in the table had just five games remaining; and, with two points awarded for a win and one point for a draw, Kilmarnock could still, theoretically, equal East Fife's points total; but the reality of the situation was that there was now no chance East Fife would be taking the drop down to the Second Division.

Just four days after the defeat to Aberdeen, East Fife were due to face Motherwell at home; and, having not set foot in Bayview since the Celtic game on 17th February, I was looking forward to the match with eager anticipation.

It was a bright and sunny but rather blustery day as I alighted from the 'bus in Leven not long after two o'clock before walking in the direction of the BawbeeBridge. However, as I had some time to spare, I decided to have a browse through the albums in Drennan's record shop in Bridge Street. My fourteenth birthday was now less than a month away, and it was time to decide what record I would be spending my birthday money on!

As I browsed through the album sleeves, the chart hit 'Tie A Yellow Ribbon' by Tony Orlando and Dawn was playing in the background. It was one of these annoying pop tunes that you just couldn't get out of your head, and certainly not what a young Hawkwind fan wanted to hear. However, as I left the shop and started walking over the BawbeeBridge and up towards Bayview, I just couldn't get the tune out of my cranium. And, rather annoyingly, the sickeningly sweet vocals of Tony Orlando and his female backing group seemed to be keeping time with the pounding of my footsteps:

"Oh, tie a yellow ribbon round the ole oak tree,

if you still want me . . . "

Eventually, I arrived at the Bayview turnstiles and paid my fifteen pence before climbing up the stairs to the top of the terracing. The gusty wind, which was coming from the west, was particularly strong at this point, and I hoped that it wasn't going to spoil the match.

When the game kicked off, East Fife were playing into the strong wind, and appeared to be struggling to get the ball under control during the opening exchanges. It was rather surprising, therefore, when, just ten minutes into the match, Doug Dailey fired a loose ball into the net after a Billy McPhee corner had been blocked by a Motherwell defender.

Despite the conditions, the home side could well have built up a three-goal advantage before half-time had Motherwell 'keeper Keith MacRae not pulled off an incredible save from a Bobby Duncan drive; and had the referee not waved away strong claims for a penalty when Walter Borthwick was clearly bundled over in the box. Then, with half-time looming, the visitors netted a disputed equaliser when inside-left Peter Miller shot home from what appeared to be an offside position.

The opinion voiced on the terraces when the half-time pies were being savoured was that East Fife's luck was out, judging by what had been witnessed during the first forty-five minutes. Much as I tried to eavesdrop on the conversations and match analysis all around me as I leaned a crush barrier at the Aberhill end of the ground awaiting the start of the second half, however, the sound of 'Tie A Yellow Ribbon' continued to drown everything else out:

"A simple yellow ribbon's all I need to set me free . . . "

When the second half got under way, the strong wind was still dictating play; but before long East Fife, and in particular goalkeeper Ernie McGarr, worked out a way that the conditions could be used to the home side's advantage.

When the opportunity arose, the ball was played back to Ernie in the home goal (the goalkeeper was allowed to pick up pass-backs in those days), who would then launch a wind-assisted punt down the park. The wind was so strong that every kick-out from the 'keeper landed inside the opponent's penalty area, which inevitably put the Motherwell goal under severe pressure. Eventually, on the hour-mark, the tactics paid off when Doug Dailey scored a second; then, ten minutes later, Billy McPhee added goal number three from the penalty spot.

By this stage of the game, Motherwell were struggling to get the ball under control and string two passes together due to the conditions, and the match eventually ended in favour of the home side by three goals to one.

When the referee's whistle sounded, I hurried out of the exit and hastily made my way along Wellesley Road, then ran down the brae and across the BawbeeBridge to catch the 'bus back up the coast. I made my way to the rear of the vehicle, where I took my seat amongst several other jubilant East Fife supporters, all of whom were obviously delighted that the first league victory since the Kilmarnock game back in January had finally been recorded.

Of course, having no mobile 'phones and internet in those days, we had to rely on one of our number having a transistor radio with them to listen to the final scores being read out at five o'clock, so that we could try to work out our latest league position.

As the 'bus made its way east towards Lundin Links, the newsreader started to read out the results, and we youngsters decided that it would be great fun trying to predict, judging by the tone of his voice, what the scores were going to be.

And so, after he had read out the home team's tally, we would shout out what we thought the away team had scored. On this particular afternoon, the results that emanated from the tinny sounding transistor radio were:

"Aberdeen nil; Dundee United . . . . ", "NIL!", we shouted.

"Airdrieonians one; Saint Johnstone. . . . ", "TWO, no, THREE!" came the shout amidst much giggling and hilarity.

"Will you lot shut up! I am trying to listen to the results!" shouted the guy with the transistor radio. But, boys being boys, we continued unabated; that is until the East Fife result came through:

"*East Fife three; Motherwell one*"; and a cheer went up amongst the black and gold bedecked passengers.

Unfortunately, all that this outburst of euphoria did was to rekindle the annoying song that had been haunting me all afternoon:

"Now the whole damned 'bus is cheerin',

and I can't believe I see;

A hundred yellow ribbons round the ole,

round the ole, oak tree . . .

dah dah dah dah dah dah dah dah"

19

It was now the school Easter holidays, which meant two weeks of utter bliss and relaxation away from the monotonous rigours of the classroom.

On the evening of the day after the Motherwell game, I chanced to overhear part of my mum's telephone conversation with her older brother, my Uncle Bert, who lived down in Gloucestershire. Mum 'phoned Uncle Bert every Sunday evening to catch up on family news.

"Well, if you're happy to have him, that would be great", I heard her say. *"It'll be a nice change for him, and he'll be less likely to get up to mischief staying with you rather than being left to his own devices at home for a fortnight".*

Who could my mum be speaking about? As soon as her telephone conversation had finished, all became clear when she shouted me through to the living room.

"How would you like to spend the rest of the school holidays with your Uncle Bert?" she asked.

My face lit up. The thought of spending over a week with my auntie and uncle down in Gloucestershire sounded just perfect. It was also rather convenient as far as East Fife's fixtures were concerned, because this coming Saturday's home game against Dundee had been postponed due to Dundee's Scottish Cup semi-final against Celtic, and the Saturday after that they would be away from home.

"That sounds great", I replied, my face grinning from ear to ear.

"Well that's it settled then", mum said, before consulting the calendar and carefully working out the logistics for my transportation to the south-west of England.

"You can travel south by train this coming Tuesday, then come back north a week on Saturday. I will take you as far as Edinburgh and put you on the train that will take you to Birmingham, where you'll have to change on to the Bristol train. You'll have to listen to all the announcements made by the guard, and also ask the ticket inspector to keep you right so that you will know when to change trains and also when the train is approaching Cheltenham, where Uncle Bert will be waiting for you".

How strange. I wasn't considered to be mature enough to travel on my own by 'bus from Cellardyke to Leven to attend a match at Bayview Park, but here I was about to embark on an eight-hour long journey through a foreign land during which I would have to change trains in the centre of the second-most heavily populated city in the country before hopefully disembarking at a railway station in the south-west of England where my uncle would be waiting anxiously.

"Yes, I am sure I can manage to do that", I excitedly assured her; although deep down I was perhaps just a little apprehensive at the daunting task set before me.

I had enormous respect for Uncle Bert. He had been a Royal Marine during the Second World War; and, at the tender age of just nineteen, had been coxswain in charge of a landing craft carrying around 200 men during the D-Day landings on the Normandy beaches in 1944. He eventually became a Marine Commando, and remained a member of the armed forces until being de-mobbed in 1946.

Bert was based for a while at HMS Jackdaw, near Crail, and it was during his time there that he met my Auntie Joan, who he married a couple of years later. To cut a long story short, my mum would never have met my dad had she not travelled up from her home in Bristol some years later to visit Joan's family in Cellardyke. It stands to reason, therefore, that if Uncle Bert hadn't survived the D-Day landings, then I wouldn't exist!

When his armed service days were over, my uncle became a policeman with Gloucestershire Constabulary, and eventually worked his way up through the ranks to become an Inspector.

Uncle Bert had a very likeable personality, but it was clear that he didn't stand any nonsense; a trait which I suppose he must have honed thanks to many years in the police force.

And so, on Tuesday 3rd April, mum drove us to Kirkcaldy, where we caught the train to Edinburgh. Shortly after pulling out of the station, we passed the ground where I had attended my first ever senior football match, Stark's Park; and, as I gazed out of the window, a panoramic view of the pitch could be had, if only for just a few seconds. There can't be many football grounds where train passengers passing on a Saturday afternoon can get to see the game for free, I thought to myself, even if it was only a brief glimpse!

At Waverley Station, mum put me on the southbound train and found me a window seat facing a rather attractive young girl, who was about the same age as myself and also travelling alone. When the train started to pull away from the platform, my mum walked alongside for as long as she could, waving enthusiastically and blowing kisses.

How embarrassing. I was nearly fourteen years old; a young teenager; and rapidly becoming more than a little interested in the opposite sex. My mum, by saying farewell in a way that would suggest I was nothing more than a child, had probably blown my chances of engaging in any sort of chat-up with the young lady sitting opposite.

Before long, we were clear of the city and racing through the verdant East Lothian countryside. Eventually, out to my left, I could make out Berwick Law; then the Bass Rock; but from an entirely different angle than what I was used to seeing from my bedroom window. What an exciting adventure!

I looked at the young girl sitting opposite me, and she looked back. I opened my mouth to speak, but just couldn't find the words or pluck up the courage. So I just turned to look out of the window again, trying to think about ways to break the ice.

Would she like football? Probably not. Would she like music?

Of course she would, but probably not the sort of music that I listened to with my pals. Heavy rock and progressive rock were the genres that we were 'into' at the time; bands like Hawkwind, Black Sabbath and Deep Purple; whereas she would more than likely have posters of David Cassidy or Donny Osmond plastered all over her bedroom wall.

A short while later, the train pulled into Berwick-on Tweed. So we were in England already? I exchanged glances with the young girl, then opened my mouth to say that I didn't think we would have travelled so far in what seemed such a short time, but the words wouldn't come. The result was that I simply gawped at her and did what must have looked like an impression of a goldfish. I decided it would be best just to look out of the window again, and try to think of an interesting topic of conversation.

After pulling out of Berwick station and crossing high over the River Tweed by way of the Border Bridge, I wondered if what I was catching brief glimpses of through the trees was Shielfield, the home ground of Scottish Second Division side Berwick Rangers. Was this the ice breaker?

I turned to face the girl in order to ask if she could see what I thought I had seen, but she was now engrossed in her 'Jackie' magazine with a 'Do Not Disturb' expression on her face. In hindsight, this was probably just as well. And that's how it continued. When she eventually disembarked at Newcastle, we still hadn't exchanged a single word.

As the train sped further south, I reflected on what might have been. What if I hadn't been so shy? What if I had struck up a conversation with her, and we had exchanged addresses and agreed to become pen pals? What if our friendship had eventually blossomed into a romantic one and she had become my girlfriend?

I nodded off with these thoughts running round in my head, and about an hour later I was awakened by the squeal of the carriage wheels negotiating a sharp bend followed by the sound of the brakes as the train slowly came to a halt.

Looking out of the window, I could see that we were in an enormous station; and, as the ticket inspector passed, I asked him if we were in Birmingham because that's where I was to change trains.

"No, this is York", he replied. *"You've got a bit to go yet, but don't worry young man, I'll let you know when we're getting close".*

I decided that it would be better to stay awake as we journeyed ever further south, and gazed out of the window as we passed through several built up areas.

From the hoardings on the side of factory buildings as we entered a particularly dense urban conurbation, I was able to work out that we were passing through Leeds, so I kept gazing out of the window, hoping to catch a glimpse of Elland Road, the Leeds United football ground.

Leeds were a great side in the early 1970's, and had been regular contenders for the English League title since having been promoted to the First Division at the end of the 1963/64 football season. They had won the first of their three English League Championship titles in 1969.

Their status in the English game had never waned during their time in the top flight, and the club currently had several prominent Scottish internationalists in their side, including the likes of Billy Bremner, Gordon McQueen, Peter Lorimer, Eddie Gray, Joe Jordan and David Harvey.

Managed by Don Revie, Leeds also had several other well known players on their books at the time, like England's Jack Charlton, Trevor Cherry and Allan Clarke; Irishman Johnny Giles and Welsh wizard Terry Yorath.

Wouldn't it be great, I thought, if the train was to pass close to the Leeds training ground and I could see these household names going through their paces? Or even better, what if the railway line ran past Elland Road in the same way that it ran past Stark's Park, which would allow me to see right inside the ground? I decided to keep my eyes peeled!

LEEDS UNITED
Eddie Gray
OUTSIDE LEFT

LEEDS UNITED
MID-FIELD
BILLY BREMNER

Unfortunately, the train never did pass Elland Road or the Leeds United training ground, and the closest I came to seeing anything of interest which might have been connected to Leeds United was when I saw what I thought must be the Elland Road floodlights some distance away.

After Leeds, the train passed through Sheffield and Derby, both of which were also home to top English sides at that time. DerbyCounty, managed by the legendary Brian Clough, were a highly respected club during the early 1970's, and were actually the reigning English League champions at the time of my train journey. They, too, had a number of highly rated Scots in their number, including Archie Gemmill, John McGovern and John O'Hare.

A short time after the train had cleared Derby, I was still gazing out of the window when I felt a tap on my shoulder. It was the ticket inspector. *"Birmingham New Street next stop"* he announced. *"We'll be there in about ten minutes".*

As the train slowed down on entering the station, I pulled my bag down from the luggage rack and made for the exit. Stepping down from the train, I looked for the destination boards to see where I had to go for the Bristol train, but it was all a bit confusing. Luckily, a kindly lady spotted my confused look; and, in a strange accent, asked me where I was heading to before pointing me in the right direction.

Once on board the Bristol train, I counted the minutes until we were due to arrive in Cheltenham; which, according to my mum, would be about an hour after leaving Birmingham. Sure enough, right on time, the train came to a halt right beside a large blue enamel sign with white lettering that proclaimed the name of the station to be 'Cheltenham Spa'.

I disembarked on to a crowded platform; looked to the left, and then to the right, where I spotted Uncle Bert's cheery face in the distance. I had safely made it to what seemed to me like one of the far corners of the earth!

DERBY COUNTY
STRIKER
JOHN O'HARE

DERBY COUNTY
MID-FIELD
JOHN McGOVERN

20

On the way from Cheltenham railway station to my uncle and auntie's house, which was situated in the small town of Churchdown, roughly half way between Cheltenham and Gloucester, Uncle Bert announced that he had some exciting news for me.

"I've been speaking to one of my police colleagues down in Bristol", he announced. *"He has a son around your age, Simon, who is a huge BristolCity fan. They have a home game this coming weekend against Carlisle United he tells me; and, if you like, I can run you down there on Saturday and you can go to the game with Simon and his dad. You can then stay the night with them, and I will come back down for you on Sunday evening. How does that sound"?*

How did that sound? It sounded just perfect!

I spent the next few days just lounging around and taking my uncle's Jack Russell terrier for a walk around the local streets. My uncle and auntie were out at work during the day and I had been left in the charge of Auntie Joan's elderly mother, Alice. There wasn't much to do, but I was enjoying the change of environment and the opportunity to explore a small town in what was, to me, a foreign land.

On the Wednesday afternoon, after returning from dog-walking duties, I had a browse through the local newspaper which was lying on the living room coffee table. Naturally, I thumbed through the pages until I came to the sports section, where I read a preview for a rugby match to be played that evening between Gloucester and Cheltenham. A local derby!

As soon as Uncle Bert arrived home from work I asked him if he liked rugby. *"Yes, it's all right, I suppose. Why do you ask"?*

I told him about the match taking place that evening; and, to cut a long story short, he eventually agreed to take me.

Rugby was still strictly an amateur sport in the early 1970's, and the Kingsholm Rugby Ground, where Gloucester's English Premiership matches are regularly broadcast live on television in the present day, was not nearly as well developed back then. The ground now has a capacity of over 16,000, most of which is seated, but in 1973 it consisted of a grandstand which ran along the length of one side, and low terracing constructed from railway sleepers on the other three sides.

The match turned out to be very one-sided, with the 'Cherry and Whites' displaying some neat passing rugby which inevitably resulted in a considerable points total being run up against a Cheltenham side who were, it has to be said, just not in the same class.

Saturday finally arrived; and, after breakfast, we headed down the motorway to Bristol. My uncle's colleague and his son Simon greeted us at the front door of their house, and almost as soon as we met I just knew that Simon and I were going to hit it off.

Shortly after lunchtime, we waved goodbye to Uncle Bert before heading across the City to Ashton Gate, City's home ground, where Simon's dad bought our tickets before heading off for a pre-match beer.

There was still about an hour to go before kick off, which gave Simon and I the opportunity to have a browse through the sizeable club shop, where I bought myself a scarf with 'The Robins' printed on one side. I was very impressed with the shop, which was like a small supermarket; and I was also impressed with the variety of merchandise on display.

As far as I knew, no Scottish football ground at the time had a facility remotely like this. There were replica jerseys for sale, as well as scarves, hats, mugs, pennants, and sports kit bags with the club crest emblazoned on the side. Match programmes from previous seasons were also on sale, and I spent several minutes rummaging through them.

BRISTOL CITY 72/73

FOOTBALL CLUB - ASHTON GATE

No. 20 — Second Division
CITY v.
CARLISLE UNITED
Saturday, April 7th — 3 p.m.

OFFICIAL PROGRAMME
INCLUDING THE FOOTBALL LEAGUE REVIEW

5p

After leaving the shop, we entered the ground through the rear of the recently constructed Dolman Stand, which was where Simon and his dad usually sat. As we were amongst the first supporters to enter the stadium that afternoon, Simon suggested that we climb up to the very rear of the grandstand before it got too busy so that I could appreciate the fantastic view.

It certainly was a great vantage point, and it seemed like we were towering high above the pitch. The main stand, on the opposite side of the ground, was also an impressive structure; and, to the left of our viewpoint, could be seen the covered terrace behind the south goal; where, according to Simon, the hardcore City supporters congregated. To our right was an uncovered terrace, where the supporters of visiting teams were usually housed. It was an impressive stadium.

By kick-off time there were over 10,000 inside the ground, and there was a good atmosphere as the game got under way; but the home supporters were silenced when Carlisle took an early lead.

The joy of the visiting team was short-lived, however, as City turned the game around to lead three-one at half-time, with one of the goals scored by Gerry Gow, a player who Simon informed me was a Scotsman like myself! A fourth goal for the home side during the closing stages of the match put the icing on the cake.

I had thoroughly enjoyed my first taste of English football, and decided that BristolCity were now going to be my second team after East Fife. City moved up to seventh place in the Second Division table thanks to this victory; but unfortunately, Simon informed me, promotion to the top tier was no longer mathematically possible with only four games left to play.

That evening, whilst Simon's mum and dad watched telly, we played Subbuteo in his bedroom. Of course, because his dad was a big a football fan, unlike my dad, Simon had all the very latest Subbuteo teams and all the best accessories. There was no need for him to fashion table football players from old shoe boxes and buttons!

The following day, there was another treat in store for me. After breakfast, we drove to Eastville, the home ground of City's rival club Bristol Rovers, where there was a weekly open air market held in the ground's car park.

I had never been to such a market before. Several stalls were selling vinyl seven inch single records at greatly reduced prices as they had now dropped out of the charts. I snapped up a couple of singles, which if my memory serves me correctly were 'In My Own Time' by Family; and Hawkwind's 'Silver Machine'.

I was disappointed at Simon's choice of 'Ooh Wakka Doo Wakka Day' by Gilbert O'Sullivan. His musical taste was obviously not as sophisticated and as well developed as mine.

After we had finished browsing through the stalls, we started to make our way back to the car, but noticed that one of the exit gates of the football ground itself was open, so we went in for a look.

As well as being a football ground, Eastville was used for greyhound racing, and the pitch was completely surrounded by an oval a dog track. The whole place had a 'higgledy-piggledy' feel about it, and looked like it had seen better days.

The terracing just inside the gate we had entered, which I was reliably informed was called the 'Tote End', was quite far back from the pitch, and the view was obstructed by numerous lighting poles which presumably illuminated the dog racing.

To our left was the tall and imposing main stand, which ran for about two-thirds the length of that side, in front of which was open terracing. To our right was a long, low grandstand; and, at the far end, there was a large oval section of open terracing. Behind this was a gas works, which Simon informed me was the reason that Rovers' unofficial nickname is 'The Gas'.

The most surprising feature of the Bristol Rovers ground, however, was the flower beds containing shrubs and roses that had been dug out of the grassed half circles behind each goal. It looked quite surreal!

"We'll probably be down here next Saturday", Simon announced as we left Eastville. *"Dad likes to spend Saturday afternoons at the football, no matter where. Pity you're going home, because you could have come with us again".*

That evening, driving back up the motorway in Uncle Bert's car, I pleaded with him to phone my mum and ask if it would be okay to delay my return north until next Sunday so that I could go to the Bristol Rovers game.

"You're better off going home on Saturday, and you know it", he replied sternly. And that was that.

21

During the week that followed, I was pretty much left to my own devices. By the time I had managed to prise myself out of bed on the Monday morning, my uncle and aunt had both left for work, leaving me under the supervision of Auntie Alice.

I decided to go for another walk and ventured as far as the local town centre, but there really wasn't much to see or do, so I decided that evening to ask Uncle Bert if it would be okay for me to catch the 'bus into Gloucester on the following day and get a lift back with him when he finished work. He said that he couldn't see any harm in me doing that, because if I did get lost in Gloucester city centre then all I had to do was ask for directions to the police station.

And so, after a shorter than usual lie-in on the Tuesday morning, I caught the 'bus into Gloucester. After having spent around an hour wandering around the city centre and browsing through some record shops, I walked into an enormous sports store which seemed to stock everything and anything related to football. I had always wanted a replica East Fife jersey, but had never seen one in the shops back home, so I reckoned that this was going to be the perfect opportunity to buy one.

However, after having unsuccessfully browsed through all the football jerseys on display, I thought I should enquire at the counter. The assistant frowned. *"East Fife? What colours do they play in?"*

"Black and gold" I retorted with an air of disbelief. How could he not know their colours? They were members of the top league in Scotland!

I decided that his ignorance must be because he wasn't really a football fan, so I thought it would be best if I elaborated.

"They used to play in black and gold stripes back in the days when my dad used to go to the games, but now they play in plain gold jerseys with a black collar and black cuffs. The shorts used to be white but now they're black. Socks are white with black at the top. But I don't want shorts or socks. All I want is an East Fife jersey. Plain gold, black collar and cuffs, with 'EFFC' embroidered on the chest. Do you have any in stock?"

The assistant stared at me for a few moments before replying that he could quite honestly say without looking in the back shop that they had no East Fife jerseys in stock; and, in all probability, they wouldn't be getting a delivery any time soon. Disappointed, I made my way back outside.

It was now well past lunchtime, so I sought out a baker's shop with the intention of buying a hot mince and onion bridie. However, for the second time in a matter of just a few minutes, I was met with a blank stare from a shop assistant. She had no idea what a bridie was!

"It's one of these", I said, pointing to what I thought was a tray of bridies behind the counter.

"Oh, you mean a pasty", she replied with a condescending smile, before putting one in a bag and handing it to me. The locals were strange people indeed. They apparently had no idea what a bridie was and they'd never heard of East Fife!

Outside, I took a bite of my bridie, but there was yet another surprise in store. It was full of potato and some other vegetable and had only about half of the meat content that you would find inside a Scottish bridie, which obviously had to be an economy measure on the part of the bakery. And to think it's the Scots who have the reputation of being mean!

Bridie finished, I had another wander around the shops before deciding to explore what lay beyond the city centre; and, before long, I found myself walking through streets of three-storey brick-built houses before eventually coming to a small park.

After resting on a bench for a few minutes, I decided it was about time I was making my way to the police station to meet my uncle as I didn't want to be late, so I carefully retraced my steps back the way I had come.

I got back to the police station in plenty of time for Uncle Bert finishing work, and waited patiently outside before he eventually appeared and we headed back to Churchdown. On the way home, he asked me what I had been getting up to, and he chuckled at my naïvety when I told him all about how I had been unable to buy an East Fife jersey and all about the incident in the baker's shop. But when I told him about going for a wander through the streets to the park and back his smile disappeared.

"If you come into Gloucester tomorrow, or any other day this week, you must promise me that you won't go wandering through those particular streets", I was told in no uncertain terms.

When I asked why, he replied that it just wasn't safe, especially for someone of my age. I never really thought much more about it at the time, and it wasn't until many years later that I discovered the reason why he had been so concerned.

Just a matter of weeks before my visit, the infamous Fred and Rosemary West had appeared at Gloucester Magistrates Court on various charges including the sexual assault of a young girl. Unfortunately, the young girl in question decided that she could not face testifying, and consequently Fred and Rose West were allowed to walk free. This was, of course, many years before the full extent of the couple's crimes came to light.

It turned out that one of the streets I had walked down that Tuesday afternoon was none other than Cromwell Street, where the Wests lived at number twenty-five. This was the address where it later transpired most of their sick and depraved sexually motivated crimes had taken place.

Years later, when Fred and Rose West were finally convicted of their crimes, pictures of the couple were shown on television during news reports, and I thought Fred West looked just a little familiar.

It sparked off a memory of the day that I had walked down Cromwell Street. I remembered that, as I was walking back in the direction of the city centre, I witnessed a heated argument between a traffic warden and a builder with a thick local accent who had parked his pick-up truck, fully laden with building materials, in an illegal position. That builder, if my memory served me correctly, had closely resembled Fred West.

Of course I cannot be absolutely certain, but in all probability it looks very much like I had passed within a few feet of one of the most notorious serial killers of all time!

22

The following morning, after breakfast, I found myself once again perusing the sports pages of the local paper, where I saw an article previewing CheltenhamTown's home Southern League match that evening. I wondered if Uncle Bert might fancy going along; and so, as soon as he got home from the police station, I popped the question.

"CheltenhamTown? You must be joking!" was his initial response. *"They're not even in the Football League. I think they play in the Southern League, and I don't think they're even in the top division of that competition!"*

Auntie Joan had overheard from through in the kitchen, and popped her head around the door. *"Oh, go on Bert. Take him to the game. It'll do you good to get out in the fresh air for a couple of hours, and you did say that you enjoyed the rugby last week".*

And so, for the second Wednesday in a row, I attended a sports event with my uncle. We entered Cheltenham's Whaddon Road ground via a narrow lane which emerged behind the south goal, and my first impression was one of surprise at the size of the grandstand.

"That's even bigger than East Fife's grandstand" I informed my uncle, who was trying his best to look interested. Although the other three sides consisted of terracing much lower than that at Bayview, I was still amazed that a non-league English football ground could have such proportions.

It wasn't as if Cheltenham had once been English League members and had dropped back down to the regional competitions. The club at this time had never actually competed at a higher level than the Southern League since their formation in 1887!

Since the 1970's, of course, they have spent several seasons in the English League, and at the time of writing they compete in League Two, the fourth tier.

It has to be said that the crowd that evening was sparse; it being quite apparent that the locals were about as apathetic towards their local side in those days as my uncle had seemed to be when I had suggested coming along.

Nevertheless, as we stood there watching the game with a light drizzle falling on us, I got the feeling that he was actually enjoying doing something other than simply sitting on his big cosy armchair in front of the telly. We were certainly enjoying each others' company, and I couldn't help but think that this is what it could be like if my dad took me to East Fife games.

That evening, my auntie had a quiet word just before I went to bed to thank me for having twice managed to drag Uncle Bert out of the house in the evenings.

"I think he's enjoyed doing something different for a change, rather than just sitting watching television. It's the sort of thing he would probably be doing a lot more often if we had a son your age", she remarked. Oh, the irony!

All too soon, it was time to return home to Cellardyke; and, on the Saturday morning, Uncle Bert took me to Cheltenham to catch the train north. Just as I was boarding, he pressed a pound note into my hand with the instructions that I was to purchase a meal in the dining car when lunchtime arrived.

I waved from the window as the train pulled out of the station, and before long the green Gloucestershire fields were flying past. I had enjoyed my wee trip south, and have to admit that I was more than a little sad to be heading back home.

A couple of hours later, hunger pangs started to develop, so I decided to make my way to the restaurant car. I found a seat at the first table I came to, just inside the door, which was all neatly laid out with knives, forks and spoons on a white table cloth.

The waiter came and took my order; and then, when I was waiting for my food to arrive, the train slowed down before coming to a halt inside a large railway station, which turned out to be Crewe.

Directly outside the window, there were crowds of youths all dressed in white lab coats, the sort that hospital doctors used to wear back in the 1970's. Most were wearing red and white scarves and 'Doc Marten' boots; and on the rear of their lab coats was emblazoned 'Doc's Devils'. It didn't take me long to work out that these were Manchester United supporters, and that the 'Doc' in question was United manager Tommy Docherty. They were all, apparently, waiting for the train to Stoke, where United were playing StokeCity in a league match that afternoon at the Victoria Ground.

It was as I was staring out of the window that I became aware of a group of teenage girls, a few years older than myself, who were also bedecked in red and white scarves and wearing Doc Marten boots. They stared back; and, being confined within the safety of the railway carriage, I decided to poke my tongue out at them. I wasn't prepared for what happened next.

Three of the girls decided that, as it appeared the departure of my train wasn't imminent, they would take the risk of hopping on board to confront me.

"Aw, look at 'im! He's gone all red", one of them remarked. *"Didn't fink we'd come on board, did ya luv?"* said another.

I didn't know what to say or do, and my cheeks were burning.

"This wot yoor 'avin'?" the third girl asked as she thrust the menu right in front of my face. I stammered that I didn't understand what she meant.

She put her face right in front of mine, then held the menu right in front of my eyes, before repeating loudly and slowly:

"THIS ... WOT ..... YOOR ..... AVIN?"

I realised then that she was asking me if this was what I was going to have for lunch; but, before I could answer, the shrill sound of the guard's whistle sounded, and to my immense relief the girls made a hurried exit.

Seeing them back out on the platform as the train slowly pulled out, I made a rude gesture in their direction, safe in the knowledge that they wouldn't dare try to get back on board.

I then turned my head around to await the arrival of my meal. However, looking down at the table which had been so neatly laid out before me, I couldn't believe my eyes. The girls had stolen every piece of cutlery from the four place settings whilst I had been distracted by the menu being thrust in front of my face!

23

On the same Saturday that I had travelled north at the end of my more than memorable trip to Gloucestershire, 14th April 1973, the boys in black and gold had travelled through to North Lanarkshire to face Airdrieonians at BroomfieldPark.

It was now two weeks since East Fife had played a league match, as their scheduled opponents for the previous Saturday's fixture, Dundee, had been otherwise engaged in a Scottish Cup semi-final clash with Celtic at HampdenPark. As that game had ended in a no-scoring draw, the two sides had to meet again on the following Wednesday evening, 11th April, which ruled out any possibility that East Fife's postponed match with the Dens Parkers could have been played on that date. As a result, the Methil men were a little short of match practice.

Going into the Airdrie fixture, East Fife were in ninth place in the eighteen-team league table, with their opponents sitting rock bottom on just thirteen points from thirty-one games played. Whilst East Fife had been idle on the previous Saturday afternoon, the 'Diamonds' had been going down heavily by five-goals-to-one against Aberdeen at Pittodrie.

Airdrie were now six points adrift of third-bottom Kilmarnock; which meant that, with just two points awarded for a win and only three games left to play, they could only draw level with the Ayrshire side if they won all their remaining matches and Kilmarnock lost all of theirs. The Broomfield club were as good as relegated.

There were now, realistically, only three teams fighting to avoid the second relegation spot; namely Dumbarton, on eighteen points with four games to go; Kilmarnock, on nineteen points with three games remaining; and Falkirk, who also had three games left, on twenty-three points.

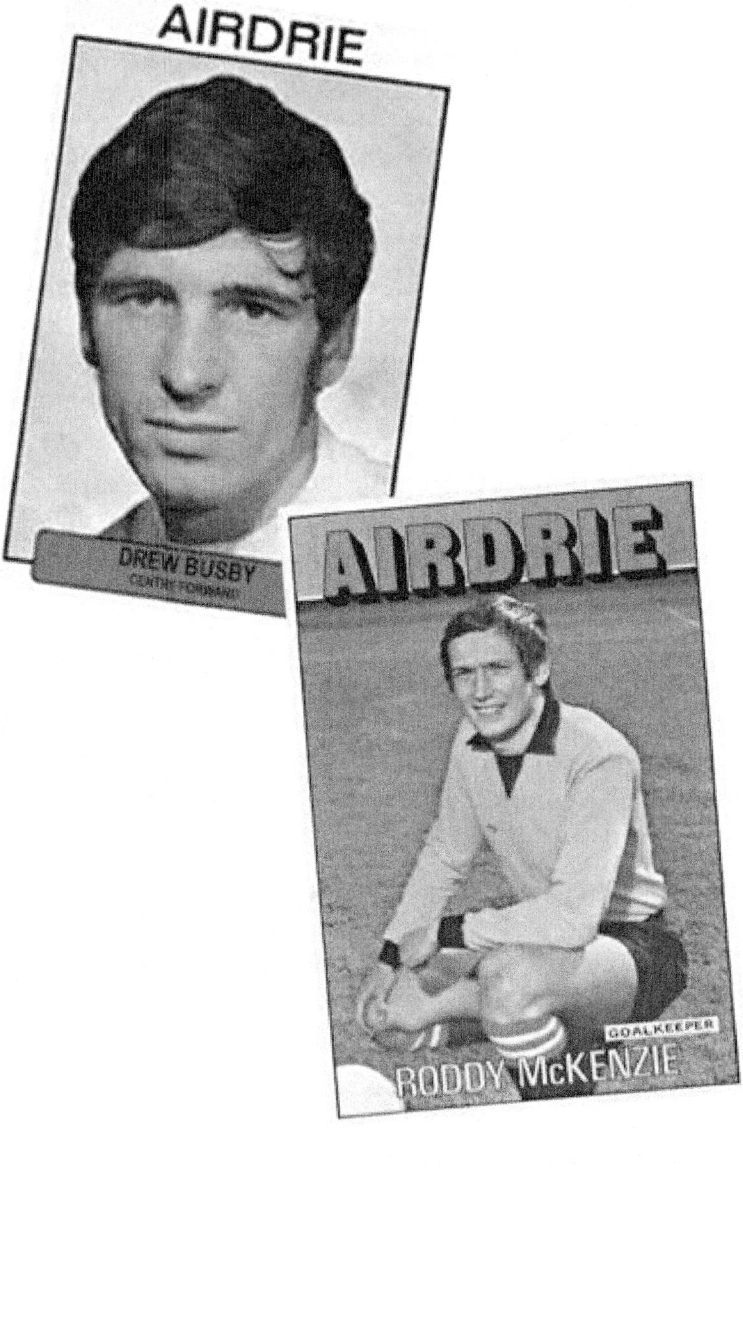
AIRDRIE
DREW BUSBY
AIRDRIE
GOALKEEPER
RODDY McKENZIE

East Fife were, of course, no longer in the relegation mix, but there was still something to play for. A top twelve finish would see the team secure a place in the following season's Texaco Cup, officially known as the International League Board Competition, which was a tournament competed for by the best Scottish teams that had not qualified for Europe, against their English counterparts.

In that respect, there were still several clubs that could pip East Fife for this honour, so it was imperative that full points were taken from their remaining matches.

The Fife got off to the best possible start at Broomfield when, during the opening exchanges, home centre-half Jim Montgomery played a pass-back too strongly in the direction of advancing 'keeper Roddy McKenzie, and the ball ended up in the Airdrie net.

There was an air of inevitability that Airdrie were destined for the drop, and it was perhaps unsurprising that their determination and play in general seemed to be lacking in purpose as the game progressed. If anything, it looked more likely that East Fife would extend their lead.

However, against the run of play, Airdrie managed to net the equaliser on the half-hour mark when Drew Busby set up Willie Hulston, who then shot neatly past the outstretched arms of 'keeper Ernie McGarr to level the game.

There was little to excite the fans during the second half; and, although some chances were created at either end, the game petered out and there was no further scoring.

However, the point gained from the one-all draw proved to be enough for East Fife to leap-frog Hearts into eighth place in the league table, as that afternoon the Edinburgh side surprisingly lost to relegation-threatened Kilmarnock at Rugby Park.

As for Airdrieonians, their fate was confirmed; but there was now going to be an almighty battle between Dumbarton, Kilmarnock and Falkirk to avoid the second relegation place!

Four days later, on Wednesday 18th April, East Fife's postponed league match against Dundee at Bayview finally got the go ahead. It was well over two weeks since I had last been to an East Fife game and I was desperate to go, but as the match had a half-seven evening kick-off it wasn't going to be possible for me to get along to Methil from Cellardyke and back at a reasonable hour using public transport.

At school on the days leading up to the game, I tried unsuccessfully to get a lift along with my East Fife supporting schoolmates and their dads, so I decided to put 'Plan B' into action. I would try to hitch a lift, as there would surely be several cars making their way from the East Neuk to Bayview for the game.

On Wednesday, after getting home from school and wolfing down my tea, I made the excuse that I was going to visit a nearby pal to discuss homework (a likely story!), before setting out along the main road heading west with my thumb extended.

Eventually I reached Pittenweem, after having walked about three miles, and was about to give up on my cunning plan when a red Ford Escort pulled up.

"Are ye gaun tae Bayview?" asked the driver.

Seated in the car were two Anster United players, who were obviously seizing the opportunity to take in an East Fife match; something they would rarely be able to do on a Saturday afternoon. It became immediately apparent that being a regular at Anster's games (when I couldn't get to Bayview) had its advantages, as the spectators were as recogniseable to the players as the players were to the spectators!

A short while later I had taken up my usual position on the Bayview terracing, in plenty of time for kick off. I could also relax in the knowledge that I had secured a return journey home after the game.

The match itself proved to be an entertaining one, despite the fact that Dundee scored what turned out to be the only goal of the game on the half-hour mark through a Billy Semple shot that crashed into the net off the underside of the bar.

After Dundee had taken that first half lead, which it has to be said was against the run of play, East Fife refused to lie down; and, for the remainder of the game, they peppered the visitors' goal with wave after wave of attack. But it was not to be their night, and my very first midweek match at Bayview ended in disappointment.

My opinion of how the match went was more than backed up in the following morning's press reports, which all stated that East Fife had been all over the Dens men right from the start; and that they should have been in front well before the visitors broke the deadlock.

"Time and again the Methil men were just wide of the mark, hitting the woodwork or the side netting" claimed the report in one national newspaper, which continued: *"Hegarty and Borthwick twice each came close in the early stages and even when they had three corners in succession the Fifers failed to produce a result".*

Never mind, it was only another three days before the next home game, against fellow Texaco Cup hopefuls St. Johnstone!

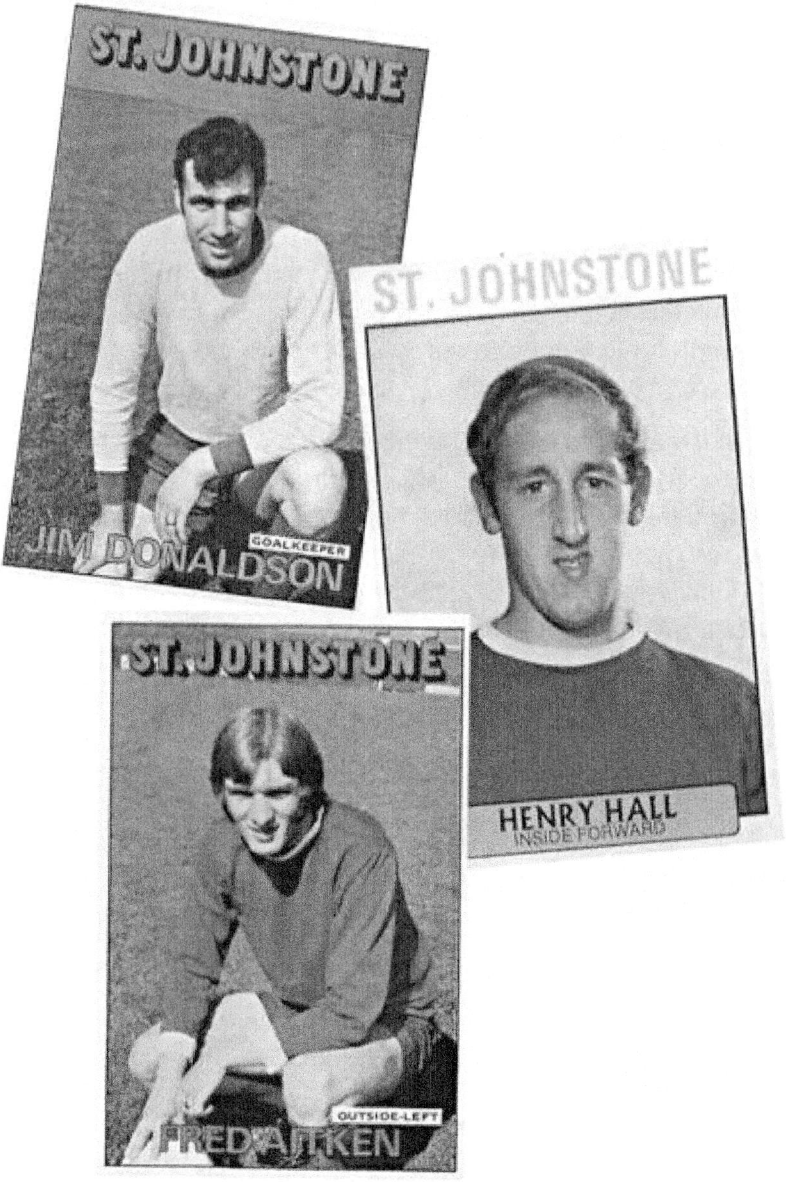
ST. JOHNSTONE
GOALKEEPER
JIM DONALDSON
ST. JOHNSTONE
HENRY HALL
INSIDE FORWARD
ST. JOHNSTONE
OUTSIDE-LEFT
FRED AITKEN

24

Despite having lost narrowly and rather unfortunately to Dundee, East Fife were still sitting in eighth place in the eighteen-team First Division table with just two league fixtures remaining, and all thoughts of relegation had long since been put to bed.

Although the Fife were still in a favourable position as far as qualification for the following season's Texaco Cup competition was concerned, they now had absolutely no chance of qualifying for the Drybrough Cup, which was a competition competed for by the four highest-scoring teams in each of the two Scottish divisions. East Fife were, in fact, one of the lowest scoring sides in the country due to their frequently used defensive style of play.

The visitors to Methil on Saturday 21st April 1973, St. Johnstone, although four places below the Methil men, were just a point behind. A home defeat would see the Perth side leapfrog their hosts, which would put East Fife's hopes of a top twelve finish and qualification for the Texaco Cup in jeopardy.

The game got off to a blistering start; and, after just twenty-five seconds play, a Johnny Love volley almost burst the net to put the Fife ahead. It was at the time the fastest-ever East Fife goal; a record that wasn't beaten until thirty-six years later when Paul McManus scored after twenty-three seconds against Queen's Park at Hampden.

I still have vivid memories of Love's lightning strike, as I was standing immediately behind the goal at the time, at the 'Bayview Bar' end of the ground. In my mind's eye I can still see the East Fife man leaping high in the air to make contact with the ball; and I can still visualise the net bulging behind the diving body and flailing arms of Saints' 'keeper Jim Donaldson.

The Fife didn't let up during the early stages of the game, and Billy McPhee doubled the advantage thanks to one of his trademark free kicks with just twelve minutes on the clock.

The game had only just re-started when Kevin Hegarty headed home what looked like number three, at which point an elderly gentleman standing to my right nudged my arm and whispered in my ear: *"Ah think wur in fur a barryload!"*

Unfortunately, Hegarty's goal was ruled out for offside; but East Fife's onslaught on the St. Johnstone goal continued unabated, with both Billy McPhee and Bobby Duncan denied by the woodwork. However, two goals inside a minute just after the half-hour mark through Henry Hall and Fred Aitken levelled the game, much against the run of play.

The second half turned out to be the complete opposite of the first, with East Fife but a shadow of the team that had started the match. Neither side created any opportunity of note during the second forty-five, and one could be forgiven for thinking that both teams were happy to settle for a draw.

As it turned out, a share of the spoils did suit East Fife and St. Johnstone, because when the final whistles sounded all around Scotland that afternoon it transpired that both sides had qualified for one of the seven Texaco Cup places up for grabs, along with Hearts, Dundee United, Ayr United, Morton and Motherwell.

There was now just one league game remaining, against Rangers at Ibrox on Saturday 28th April. The race for the 1972/73 Scottish League Championship had come right down to the wire, with Celtic topping the table going into the last round of matches on fifty-five points and Rangers just a point behind.

Celtic, having a vastly superior goal difference, were firm favourites to clinch the title, and in reality needed just a point against Hibs at Easter Road. If Celtic lost, however, any sort of victory for Rangers over East Fife would see the Championship flag flying over Ibrox.

Having no feelings either way for the 'Old Firm', of course, I wasn't in the least bit interested in the battle for the league title. Anything other than a defeat for my favourites would be a welcome result at the end of a memorable season, but as far as I was concerned there wasn't much left to play for.

During the days leading up to that final Saturday, it came to my notice that East Fife's final reserve game of the season, against their Rangers counterparts, was to be played at Bayview on Friday 27th April, the eve of the Ibrox match.

Would it be possible for me to take the 'bus to Leven and get back to Cellardyke at a reasonable hour? It wasn't a school night, I reasoned, and I would therefore be allowed to stay out later. I could also leave well before the end of the game if necessary.

By Friday tea-time I had managed to convince myself that the plan was a feasible one, and duly boarded the six o'clock 'bus to Leven. Having celebrated my fourteenth birthday on the previous day, I was now no longer eligible for a child fare, but I had no intention of paying the adult price just yet. Unfortunately, my hopes took a knock when I boarded the 'bus to find that the conductress was an old family friend.

Once I had taken my seat, she made her way up the aisle towards me with her ticket machine slung over her shoulder. *"A half to Leven",* I said, trying to raise the pitch of my voice slightly whilst staring at the floor in the hope that I wouldn't be recognised.

"A half? Now then, Jimmy, let me think", the conductress replied. *"You're exactly a week older that oor Johnny, and he's fourteen next Thursday!"*

As she produced the ticket with two swift turns of the handle on her machine, I was told in no uncertain terms: *"Ye'd better frame it, because it's yer last!"*

The reserve game turned out to be an entertaining but somewhat fiery encounter, in which Drew Noble opened the scoring for East Fife before Billy Gillies added a second to give the home side a comfortable half-time lead.

In the second half, the game boiled over, and goal scorer Noble blotted his copy book by getting himself sent off. Three Rangers players also found their way into the referee's book as they tried to fight their way back into the game, but the Ibrox second-string's efforts were in vain and ten-man East Fife held out for the win.

As for the game at Ibrox, the Methil men adopted defensive tactics during the first half in order to thwart what was surely going to be an onslaught by the Rangers forwards as they desperately tried to end the season on a high.

The defensive approach to the match seemed to be paying off as the first half progressed, with Ernie McGarr being rarely troubled thanks to a stubborn East Fife rearguard. Skipper Davie Clarke and centre-half John Martis were immense; and, time after time, they successfully managed to break down the Rangers attacks before their strikers could pull the trigger. However, midway through the first-half, Rangers broke the deadlock when a high ball into the penalty area from Derek Parlane found Quinton Young, who netted from close range. Just a few minutes later the game was as good as put to bed when AlfieConn ran on to a through ball before firing home.

Almost simultaneously, news filtered through from Easter Road that Dixie Deans had put Celtic ahead at Easter Road, and the atmosphere at Ibrox became rather subdued. The game petered out during the second half and there was no further scoring; whereas at Easter Road further goals from Kenny Dalglish and Dixie Deans quashed any lingering doubts about where the league flag was heading.

And so that was how East Fife's 1972/73 league campaign came to an end, but the season wasn't quite over yet. On the Monday following the Rangers game, the team flew out to Denmark for a three game continental tour, during which Danish club Horsens were beaten by five goals to one before fellow countrymen Aarhus were defeated two-nil. The trip was wound up with a four-three victory over German side Barmbek Uhlenh in Hamburg.

On their return to Scotland, there was no time for respite, because on the following day, Monday 7th May, Wolverhampton Wanderers visited Methil to take part in a benefit match for long serving players Dave Clarke, Dave Gorman, Walter Borthwick and Peter McQuade.

Unsurprisingly, considering their hectic schedule, it was a tired East Fife who lined up against a Wolves side who included in their number Scottish internationalist Jim McCalliog and Irish internationalist Derek Dougan.

The visitors, who had just finished their league campaign as the fifth-best placed side in England as well as having reached the semi-final of the League Cup during the season just ended, also put up a disappointing performance on the night in front of an equally disappointing crowd of 3,379; and the end result was a no-scoring draw.

"As a game is was, in honesty, a flop. No goals, no excitement, and nothing to commit the proceedings to the memory bank", was about as much as the following morning's press had to say on the match.

It was a disappointing end to East Fife's best season for many a long year, and it's perhaps just as well that I didn't make the effort to attend, because my memories from those heady days are of exciting matches played in a great atmosphere with thousands lining the Bayview terraces. I can still vividly recall these games as if they happened only yesterday, and my memories have been with me now for over half-a-century.

I doubt if I will ever again witness such exciting times watching the men in black and gold; and will conclude by saying that those nostalgic times were, quite simply, some of the best days of my life!

WOLVERHAMPTON WANDERERS
Jim McCalliog
INSIDE RIGHT

EAST FIFE
DAVID CLARKE

Epilogue

Sadly, East Fife's top-flight status was to last just one more season. Despite sitting third from the bottom of the table after all thirty-four matches of their 1973/74 league programme had been completed, they were leapfrogged by Clyde; who, against the odds, managed to take a point from each of their two outstanding fixtures against Hibs and Hearts.

Ironically, the Fife recorded their one and only competitive away victory over Rangers at Ibrox during that fateful campaign; and, towards the end of the season, it looked like the men in black and gold might be good enough to escape the drop down to Division Two. But it was not to be.

As for the Texaco Cup competition, the first round of which was played during the early weeks of the 1973/74 season, East Fife fell at the first hurdle thanks to an embarrassing 10-2 aggregate defeat at the hands of Burnley.

On a happier note, Scotland did qualify for the 1974 World Cup after beating Czechoslovakia 2-1 at Hampden on 26th September 1973. At the finals, held in West Germany during the summer of 1974, they gave a good account of themselves, but unfortunately exited the tournament at the end of the first group stage on goal difference to both section winners Yugoslavia and second-placed Brazil despite remaining unbeaten in the three games played.

As for England, they failed to qualify for the 1974 finals, so had no other option but to harp on about 1966 for yet another four years. As it turns out, that's still the only major success they have to boast about, and that's why the English media, like a broken record, relentlessly remind us of their rather fortunate win to this very day. And of course, had VAR been around in 1966, they probably wouldn't have anything to brag about at all!

My favourite English team at the start of season 1972/73, Liverpool, went on to win the English League Championship following a keenly-fought battle with Arsenal, and also won the UEFA Cup.

As for Bristol City, who I adopted as my new favourite English team towards the end of the 1972/73 season, the 'Robins' managed to end their league campaign in a very creditable fifth place in the Second Division. Three years later, in 1976, the Ashton Gate side finally won promotion back to England's top-flight after an absence of sixty-five years, where they remained for four seasons until being relegated in 1980. I still follow the results of both Liverpool and BristolCity.

It's now over fifty years since East Fife played league football amongst Scotland's elite, and it now looks very much like these days will never be seen again. I have continued to follow the club during the intervening years, when family and work commitments have allowed, and I am proud to say that in 2003, East Fife's centenary year, I wrote and published the club's centenary history; 'On That Windswept Plain'. It seems like all that 'useless information' that my dad claimed I was filling my head with actually had a purpose after all!

In more recent times I published 'Black and Gold and Blue', which details the history of the East Fife players who pulled on the dark blue jerseys of Scotland.

Thanks to my writing experience and knowledge of the club's history, I was invited to join the match programme writing team at the beginning of the 2006/07 season, and it was through my involvement with this publication that I was appointed official club photographer. It is a position that I held for twelve seasons, and it is one that I enjoyed immensely.

During my years as club photographer, I was asked to work occasionally for the press; and, as well as regularly featuring in the local East Fife Mail, my action photographs appeared in national newspapers such as The Scotsman; the Sunday Post; the Sunday Mail; and the now defunct News of the World, to name but a few.

And as for my dad, he never did set foot in BayviewPark again.

Acknowledgements

Once again I am indebted to my friend and lifelong East Fife supporter Donald Walker for some sound advice and for sharing his knowledge of the club's history on the few occasions when my own historical records were found to be lacking.

I would also like to mention another friend and lifelong East Fife fan, Joyce Anderson, for encouraging me to publish these recollections of the 1972/73 football season in the form of this book.

I should also point out that, although I have mostly clear memories of the matches that I attended that season, some of the finer details are a little blurred. I am therefore indebted to the British Newspaper Archive, from which I was able to access match reports, results and league positions from the 1972/73 campaign through the medium of certain local and national newspapers.

As for the football picture cards used in this book, they were all produced by a company called A&BC, which went out of business some fifty years ago. Despite numerous lines of enquiry, which included contacting various companies who I was advised had possibly inherited copyright of the images, my efforts to ascertain ownership of copyright were fruitless. After having then sought further advice from a number of individuals who had knowledge on such matters, I decided to take the bold step of going ahead with publication despite this uncertainty.

Similarly, the programme covers used were originally produced by the Artigraf Printing Company in Buckhaven, which also went defunct several years ago. The photographs used on the programme covers are the work of my fellow former East Fife club photographer Ricky Janetta, who has kindly granted permission for their use.

EAST FIFE
JOHN MARTIS
CENTRE HALF

EAST FIFE
RIGHT-BACK
BOBBY DUNCAN

Suggested Further Reading

If you enjoyed this book, you might also enjoy the following publications from Wast-By Books, all of which are available (unless indicated) in both paperback and Kindle eBook format from:

Amazon.co.uk

On That Windswept Plain: the First 100 Years of East Fife Football Club
(James K. Corstorphine, 2003)
ISBN: 9781976888618

Black and Gold and Blue: The East Fife men who pulled on the Scotland jersey
(James K. Corstorphine, 2022)
ISBN: 9798817263855

The Earliest Fife Football Clubs
(James K. Corstorphine, 2018)
ISBN: 9781980249580

Our Boys and the Wise Men: The Origins of Dundee Football Club
(James K. Corstorphine 2020)
ISBN: 9798643521549

East of Thornton Junction: The Story of the FifeCoast Line
(James K. Corstorphine, 1995)
ISBN: 9781976909283

Suggested Further Reading (continued)

Wrecked on Fife's Rocky Shores: Dramatic Nineteenth Century Tales of Shipwreck from around the Coast of Fife
(James K. Corstorphine, 2021)
ISBN: 9798759568513

Dyker Lad: Recollections of Life in an East Neuk of Fife Fishing Village
(Alexander 'Sonny' Corstorphine, 2018)
ISBN: 9781981019137

The Saturday Sixpence: A Selection of short stories set in a fictional Scottish seaside town during the 1960's
(James Kingscott, 2020)
ISBN 9798556376090

A Selection of Poems by 'Poetry Peter' Smith, the Fisherman Poet of Cellardyke
(Compiled by James K. Corstorphine, 2000)
ISBN: 9798644727827

The History of Steam and the East Fife Fishing Fleet
(PAPERBACK ONLY)
(Peter Smith, 1998)
ISBN: 9798767970773

All of the above titles are available in both Paperback and Kindle eBook formats (unless indicated) from:

amazon.co.uk

Just one more thing before you go . . .

Your opinion would be very much appreciated!

I would be most grateful if you could find a few minutes to rate this book on Amazon.

I will take the time to read any comments made, and any suggestions as to how I can improve the publication will be taken on board.

Thank you!

James K. Corstorphine

Printed in Great Britain
by Amazon